THE RETURN

OF THE

PRODIGAL

THE INITIATE'S ASCENT

OF THE

MIDDLE PILLAR

DOLORES ASHCROFT-NOWICKI

1

Library and Archives Canada Cataloguing in Publication

Title: The return of the prodigal : the initiate's ascent of the middle pillar / Dolores Ashcroft-Nowicki
Names: Ashcroft-Nowicki, Dolores, author.
Identifiers: Canadiana 20210116188 | ISBN 9781896238265 (softcover)
Subjects: LCSH: Occultism. | LCSH: Prodigal son (Parable) | LCSH: Spiritual life. | LCSH: Mysticism | LCSH: Self-actualization (Psychology)
Classification: LCC BF1999 .A84 2021 | DDC 130—dc23

TWIN EAGLES PUBLISHING
Box 2031
Sechelt BC
V0N3A0
pblakey@telus.net
604 885 7503

DEDICATION

To the **Sisterhood of the Violet Flame** with my love, and eternal gratitude for their support, strength, and shared laughter.

ACKNOWLEDGEMENTS

To Carol and Steven Lomax:

My love and thanks for the support and meticulous editing, without you it would not have been possible.

Love and thanks also to Chris Hill for the incredible cover illustration. Your talent always amazes me.

FOREWORD

The Story of the Prodigal Son is something most people learn in school, though it seems that modern schools, especially those with pupils from many different backgrounds, no longer consider religion as a subject. But the basis of the story is universal, the teenager wanting to leave home and set the world on fire… but needing parental permission and financial help, to do so. So off they go into the wide world and at first it is exciting and "friends" soon gather round eager to share the bounty that seems to be handed around.

But lack of experience, and reliance on those out for what they can get soon begins to take its toll. The "wild child" soon begins to find out the reality of life… the hard way. When at long last the money runs out and so-called friends drift away, loneliness, hunger, and deprivation begin to replace the excitement and the feeling of being in charge of one's life. Only when one has reached the depths can you appreciate what was once taken for granted.

Most bible stories hold the much deeper truth/realisation/ teaching concealed within them. For those of us who seek to understand the eternal question of…

WHY ARE WE HERE?

Stories hold answers and teachings, be it a parable or a fairy story, and The Prodigal Son is just one of many. What does it teach? The story of humanity and its climb from savagery to the stars is a map that shows a way back once we have learned the lesson. The prodigal had to leave in order to find the way back. It's uncomfortable, humiliating, and full of self-doubt but it's there.

Evolution is a school of hard knocks and every life form goes through it.

Every living creature existing in this time, this NOW, has got to this point by evolving. By growing in wisdom, adapting to different climates, ways of living, and coping with crises of every kind. Life itself is a prodigal... learning what forms, foods, habitats, and climates can be used, developed, grown and shared. Compare how early humanity emerging from the disappearing Ice Age, with an ordinary everyday human being in the twenty first century. YET! We are still, in one sense of the word... on the way HOME. We have a long way to go yet, before we reach the peak of what we CAN achieve. But at least the story of the Prodigal offers hope, an incentive to keep trying, keep learning, keep going forward and upward.

CHAPTER ONE

THE SPHERE OF MALKUTH

The Sphere of Reality

Malkuth is the world of manifestation and as such it is the dimension of humankind. This is where we live, move, and have our being. It is our place of evolvement where we have grown into the creative and inquiring life form we are now. During the time we have existed on this planet we have changed a great deal from an animal with animal instincts seeking to exist just long enough to reproduce ourselves before following all life into the darkness from which we emerged.

But during that far off time something changed us. Something flared into life brought about by a force higher and finer than the one driving the primitive Homo habilis, and Homo sapiens sprang into focus. Change is essential to all life forms, we adapt and change to external and internal influences and become more than we were or less as the case maybe. In the case of humankind the change was far reaching and beyond anything that could have been imagined. But Malkuth remains a place where we live out the time allotted to each of us. But, we can extend our experience of it to include four very different levels. The level of Assiah, the densest level of all, the level of Yetzirah, or the Astral, the level of Briah, which is that of the mental world, and finally the level of Atziluth or the Spiritual world. Each level has its own powers, attributes, and lessons for us to learn from and experience.

The Road of the Prodigal is the name I have always given to the Middle Pillar of the three that comprise the basis of the Qabalistic Mandala we know as The Tree of Life. Each Pillar supports a selection of Spheres or Sephiroth, three on each of the two side Pillars and five on the central Pillar. Those that concern us on this particular journey to the Light are in order of ascent, Malkuth, the Sphere of Earth and what we think of as the Real World. Yesod, the Lunar Sphere of Dreams, Imagination, and Magic. Tiphereth, the Solar Sphere of Service and Sacrifice. Daath, the Invisible and intriguing Sphere of Truth and Integrity. Kether, the Sphere of Primal Emanation. A Sphere exists on each of these four levels simultaneously and all the levels affect the one above it and the one below it in different ways.

All the journeys you are about to undertake will cause changes within you, some more than others. You will never be quite the same person who started out, but along the way you will learn a lot about yourself, and maybe a little about the people around you. It is time to begin the first journey. Keep a notebook and pen with you and always record what you have seen, heard and experienced after each session.

Malkuth in Assiah

This is the world of the five senses, each of which is a window into our physical brain, but these windows need cleaning on a regular basis. This journey begins with an actual physical experience. Put a small notebook and a pen in your pocket and go out into the nearest park or place where there are trees, grass, wild flowers, birds and hopefully some small wild life. If it is warm enough, take off your shoes and walk barefoot. Choose a time when there will be few people about, slow down the pace at which you walk and begin to notice what is around you. The first sense is sight; what can you see? Stop and pause, look around you and try to notice the smaller things as well as the obvious. Write it all down. Look for detail, the ant carrying off a leaf, a beetle on a tree root or an oddly shaped stone.

Look at the sky, clouds, and the patterns light makes as it filters through the branches and note it all down.

The Qabalah gives colour to the spheres at each level. As this course is for those of an advanced level these colours should already be known to you.[1] The colours for Malkuth in Assiah are as follows. Black rayed with yellow. To take these colours with you into the exercise wear something black and add a splash of yellow in the form of a ribbon or a flower.

Now move to the sense of sound. What can you hear? Bird song, wind, the faint noise of traffic, a plane, voices? Sing out a note, shout your name, whistle, or stamp your feet. Try to capture the sound in your inner ear. Now try for the sense of smell, the most evocative of all the senses. There are so many different scents. Grass smells different if taken from earth round the root of a tree or a bush or from a lawn. Different leaves have distinctive smells. A bird's feather may hold a faint trace of its body odour. Crush leaves and grasses between your hands and inhale the scent. Try to catch the smell of the world close by, petrol, smoke, a trace of perfume. Record it all.

How about taste; closely aligned to scent it can leave traces in the air for you to recognise. Can you recall the taste of an apple, or coffee or fresh baked bread. Grass, leaves, wild herbs, even the wind, have a taste. Finally touch; feel the earth under your feet, the roughness of tree bark, or the smoothness of a flower petal. The shape of a fallen seed, nut, or root. Run your hands over the ground and feel its shape under the covering of grass, roots, and fallen leaves. Write it all down and then turn for home. Do this for several days, each day at a different time and compare the changes in your notes.

---

1 The colours of the Middle Pillar in the Four Worlds are to be found in the Appendix at the end of this book.

Malkuth in Assiah – Working

Now you have felt the real earth, try to recall it in the mind. Try to recreate in Malkuth in Assiah in your mind. Sit quietly in a slightly darkened room with no distractions. If need be use earplugs and a sleep mask. Build in your mind's eye the walks you have taken at the times you have taken them. Build slowly and carefully the feeling, and the quality of light. Recreate the feel of the clothes you wore and the thoughts you had as you walked. Recall the things you saw and visualize them as exactly as you can. The physical brain cannot tell the difference between what is imagined and what is real so it will give you the same feelings you had when you walked for real.

Now try to re-create the sounds you heard. Don't hurry, just let them rise up. Use your notes to help you if you forget. Listen to yourself singing, shouting, and whistling. The sound of twigs and branches as they break under your feet. Bird song, animal noises, and the wind in the trees, everything you heard while walking create it again in your inner ear.

Now turn to the sense of smell. This is the most difficult of the five and you may have to work hard at this. Your organ of smell is the only one of the five that is directly joined to the brain without the need of a junction point, but it is the most difficult to recall internally.

Now recall the sense of touch, feel the coolness of the grass beneath your bare feet, the feel of rough tree bark. The smoothness of stone or the feel of rain on your face. Recall it as clearly as you can. Don't worry if you feel you can't do this as well as you had hoped the first time, you will improve as you go along. When you have done as much as you can try for the sense of taste.

Above all try to recall the space, the feel of being in nature the wonder of it, the strangeness, as if you are seeing it all for the first time. You are connecting with the Earth in its oldest and most primitive form. To be alone in such a space in the early dawn or the quietest moments of sunset is to know what it was like in the time of your ancestors. At such times you own the world, just you alone. Earth and all its treasures are yours for just a few minutes. Time is absolute here, encapsulated inside your memories. Here all time and times become one and there is no division to blind you to the gradual changes that occur in real, everyday, Malkuth time. Here you can stretch a single moment into an eternity and observe its innermost secrets. Within such a time-locked space you can insert your hand into the heart of a tree and touch its heartbeat. Or see into the centre of a fallen hazel nut and see the full-grown tree it will be.

Look at the trees and see the indwelling Dryad, the life force of the tree, within. Green and gold in colour and with a body that matches the actual tree shape. The branches are held out and up with massive strength and if you look down you can see the roots spreading out like veins, digging deep into the earth and feeding from her breast. Left to themselves such trees will stand for hundreds of years watching the moving creatures like ourselves pass into the shadow of the years.

Allow ten to fifteen minutes to recreate your walk, then return to the physical world. Never get up right away, sit quietly and let the physical world catch up with you. A drink or a snack will help to close you down. What is the value of Malkuth in Assiah? It will teach you to observe the world about you, to see it as an actuality rather than something that is just there. The world you see about you every day is there because we all believe it is there and in the form we have come to expect. When we begin to observe it more closely we see things we have not seen before simply because we did not "think of them" so they did not form part of our idea of the world about us.

Repeat the visualization several times, at least once for each of the different times of day you did the real thing. Keep up the practice of noticing the world about you. Carry a camera in your pocket as well as a notepad and pen. Train yourself to note down anything you see that seems out of the ordinary. Professional photographers are experts at this.

You can augment this exercise by practising the recalling of different scents, sounds, voices, and musical instruments. Touching and recalling surfaces, from satin to sand paper, tastes both sweet and sour, sharp and acid. This will affect your senses in the everyday world by sharpening your ability to recognise faces, recall names, and remember places by familiar buildings and distinctive landmarks.

Malkuth in Yetzirah

You will find that the exercises of the first level will help you here. This is because you will be able to recall places, feelings, sights and sounds more clearly than before. You will need to do something actual and practical to prepare for the internal experience. If the time of year is right begin by looking at gardens. Small ones, big ones, elegant landscaped ones and ordinary municipal parks.

Walk through them and observe how they are constructed, note the kinds of flowers used to fill different kinds of areas. See how trees and bushes are used to draw attention to certain places, to give height or fill in an awkward shape between two paths. Note the play of colour and shadow and how different shades of the same colour can add definition. A good gardener uses colour and types of flower with the same skill as an artist. See how the eye can be drawn first to one side of a path and then the other, how certain arrangements of colour and placing make you pause to stand and stare.

Flowers and gardens provide homes and sustenance for insects and small creatures that, like us, have evolved on Earth and must be acknowledged as her children. They make their homes and forage in the brightly coloured blooms and live in a secret scented world we can never know... or, can we?

If it is wintertime and the gardens are sleeping, then turn to books and magazines and fill your mind and eyes with colour in seed catalogues, or books of famous gardens and parks. Now it is time to enter the world of Malkuth in Yetzirah, the astral world of Earth.

Malkuth in Yetzirah – Working

Sit quietly in a place where you will not be disturbed and where you are comfortable being neither too warm nor too cool. Close your eyes and fill your mind with flowers, colours and scents. Hold in your mind's eye a gate of delicately wrought iron set into a high wall of polished granite. Beyond the gate you can see a pathway of smooth stone edged with tall Yew trees trimmed into elegant oval forms. Laid out before the gate is a robe in the colours of Malkuth at this level, citrine, olive, russet and black and with it a cord of yellow, put on the robe and stand before the gate. It opens silently inviting you into The Garden.

The main path opens out onto a central area of green grass edged with small flowers of every colour. In the centre stands a life-sized bronze statue of Pan the goat foot god of Nature in all its forms. His hair sweeps back from a broad brow and his neatly trimmed beard frames his mouth and chin. The ram's horns are curled into sturdy half circles and lie close to the head. Half standing, half leaning against a marble pillar in one hand he holds his pipes and in the other a silver cup half filled with wine. The goat limbs do not seem out of place here, and the half smile seems to understand your acceptance.

From this small circle of green other paths lead off, each offering a new vista of colour, scent, and the promise of hidden surprises. Choose a path, any path for they will all come together in the end. This garden is your secret place, your idea of earth as it is on the astral or Yetziratic level. It will reflect your idea of beauty as a growing living thing. Every flower is a smile, a laugh a moment of happiness that you have experienced in your life. When you see a wilting blossom, or one that is broken it is a symbol of something that has hurt or disappointed you. But while you are here, you can choose to see what you want to see.

Look, here is a beehive set in the middle of a mass of flowers; the bees are giddy with their scent and the promise of their bounty. Hold out your hand and watch as a honeybee settles on it. It preens its wings and strokes its antennae before setting off on its search. Follow it with your eyes, and then wish yourself into its tiny black and golden body.

The garden changes immediately, you now see it through faceted eyes; the colours are extended beyond the human range, as are the scents. Both give you information as to range, direction, type of pollen and volume. Your wings hum with power vibrating many hundreds of times a second. Ahead of you is a strange geometric shape but it holds the promise of a rich harvest. You plunge into its centre and the smell of the pollen is overwhelming. With quick movements your forelegs gather the harvest and attach it to your hind legs. Then you emerge to find another larder.

Again and again you descend into the heart of each flower, plundering its sweetness but also paying the price nature demands in the dusting of pollen that covers your body. As you fly from feast to feast you spread the DNA of each bloom and Mother Earth mixes and matches the results.

Before you looms the hive and the other workers swarm about you brushing off the treasure you have carried back and storing it. You dance your memory of the pathway to the flowers and watch as others fly off to follow your directions. You hover over the hive and move back to slowly return to

13

your own form.

"That was well done." You turn and see before you Pan, no longer a statue but flesh and blood, as much as this is possible at this level. He is taller than you thought, but his golden eyes hold nothing but humour and kindness.

"Walk with me."

Under the warm sun you both walk through The Garden. Pan points out the Herbs scenting the air with their spicy perfumes, and the places where vegetables are grown for they also add colour to the whole. He takes you to a pool and points to the lotus flowers, some blue, some white pink tipped. He smiles as you bend closer to take in their scent… you feel a slight push in your back and tumble head over heels into the water sinking down and down into the rich silt at the bottom of the pool.

You feel the change coming over you and flow into it without fear. The silt encloses you and as a seed you rest in it and send out tiny filaments of green to feed and grow strong. You have no sense of time or urgency, everything moves at the pace designed for it. The filaments become stronger and dig down into the nutrients below you to become roots. At the same time there is within you a longing for warmth and light and from the seed there emerges a slender stalk that begins to push upwards towards another environment, as yet unknown but longed for.

At the tip of the stalk there grows a swelling that becomes more pronounced as its stem strengthens. Far above there is light, warmth and a new form to be assumed. The swelling becomes a tightly sealed bud filled with beauty soon to be unveiled. The surface of the pool is breached, warmth and light touch the bud and it opens slowly to reveal in inner beauty of the lotus flower, its scent is released into the air as it opens and you sit in the centre, new born as a sun Child within the Lotus.

Pan reaches down and takes your hands and lifts you from

the pool on to dry land, smiling. For you a lifetime as a seed, a plant and a flower have passed, but in the garden the sun has only just begun to turn towards its setting. With Pan you walk further into the garden to a place beneath the shade of a tree. There a simple meal has been laid out, bread, honey, cheese, wine, fruit. As you eat he plays and at the sound of his pipes the younger brethren begin to gather. They sit, lie, stand and nestle against Pan who is their version of God and their Guardian. A mother deer brings her fawn to be blessed, a mole sits at his hoofed feet and looks up at him adoringly. An elderly dog, limping on arthritic limbs seeks a place at his side where his pain is eased. Rabbits, birds, even snakes and insects gather to be in his presence, seeking the touch of his hand, feeding from his fingers. You are surrounded by them, accepted because you are with him.

"You may come here when you will," Pan tells you. *"I will not always be here, I have many responsibilities, but I will come when I can. You built this place to be your sanctuary, and I will fill it with love."*

He rises to his feet, his shaggy limbs graceful in movement. The animals gather close for a last touch of his hand. With a gentle smile he passes his palm over the old dog sleeping at his feet and the worn out form turns, and from it rises the young dog that was, the old form remains in the garden and will decay into it. But the renewed form will go with its beloved Master into a new life.

"There is still much for you to explore here, you have seen only a small part of it, and you can build more as and when you will." Pan melts into the landscape and you are alone.

You make your way back to the centre of the garden the statue stands as before. Make your way back along the path to the gate and it will open for you and close behind you. You look back through the gate to the beauty beyond and know that this is of your own making; this is Earth as it should be, wild, free, beautiful and peaceful.

15

Your own time and place awaits you in Malkuth in Assiah return now and wake slowly and in peace, but knowing that this "other world" will always be there for you to rest in and draw comfort and energy.

Malkuth in Briah

It is how we think of the earth around us that creates that world, and as we all think differently, we all create our own version of it. A farmer thinks of Earth in terms of produce, a scientist in terms of technology, a writer or an artist as a blank page or a canvas on which to depict their view of what they see, hear, or imagine going on around them. Then there are the un-awakened ones. They experience the world as others see it and they allow them to do so because it is less trouble and less hassle than building their own concept of it.

As I have said and written on numerous occasions, thought is a creative power that all human beings share. The world changes as they change and re-arrange their ideas of it. We now accept air travel, computers, mobile phones, and television, things that would have been magical 300 years ago. But gradually through small but important changes in the way we think, all those things have come into being, and are now accepted.

Briah is the level where we can communicate with the Archangelic world and in the sphere of Malkuth this will be Sandalphon. This Being has responsibility for this earth and its life forms as well as the elemental life under its ruler Ghob. Elements like everything else in our universe are composed of particles and they have a life force of their own. It may not be like ours, but it has existence and sentience and so deserves to be acknowledged. Once we do this we can begin to forge a relationship with things we have previously thought of as being inanimate. Life, animation and intelligence can take many forms and on many levels, do not discount them or their existence.

We fill the Briatic dimension of Earth with thoughts of gloom and doom, of war and strife, of dissension and fear and in doing so we create such things. If instead we all decided to think about finding a new source of power, or a way to explore space and find new planets to colonise, or of finding ways to live together without trying to change others to our way of thinking because we think their way is wrong...we could bring about those changes. But to do that would mean giving up the belief that we alone have the right to tell others what to do and how to think. What has saved us from total disaster up to now is the fact that every now and then certain people are born who introduce new ideas new inventions, new trains of thought that avert confrontation, for a while!

The old challenges that once diverted us have gone and this planet is now an open book. There are no new places to explore, mountains to climb, even the oceans are giving up their secrets. There are just two areas left, two spaces... the space without, meaning the planets, the solar system and beyond, and the inner space within us. Both are reachable, both offer new openings, experiences and rewards. Both will take courage and determination.

The exploration of space is close; we have already begun to see the promise of what lies "out there" and its rewards of knowledge, new life forms and the challenges of a new way of life. But the same is true of the exploration of inner space, a space that is equally vast, and equally demanding of courage and equally dangerous if not prepared for in advance. It is this inner space that we are exploring in this series of lectures and guided workings, and as we make our way through the five energy centres that make up both the physical and the spiritual spine hopefully we will be able to release those energies and learn to use them.

The old adage tells us that "necessity is the mother of invention". It is an unpalatable truth that many of the things we use in this modern life have come about through inventions made during times of war. Among them we find radar, communication devices, and new medical and surgical techniques to name but a few. Evolution advances through the medium of making mistakes until we find out what is causing them and rectifying them. It is painful to realise that conflicts, more often than not, stimulate the human mind to seek out and correct such mistakes.

We speak of world peace as something we desire but we think of it being well-nigh impossible. But many human beings see the state of Inner Peace as being more easily attainable and it seems like less work!

What kind of location do we usually think of as being peaceful? Well we all have different ideas about this, but without a doubt the one place where we feel SAFE, is home. Home is where we can kick off our shoes shed the office suit, the tie, the high heels, and the professional "face" we all wear in public. But even here we feel constrained to certain habits and ways, and there are always interruptions and calls upon our time. To be deeply and safely at peace we need to create a location within our own mental dimension. So let's begin to do that.

Choose a chair with a firm back and place a rolled up towel in the lumber region and another and smaller one just behind the neck. Elevate the feet with a cushion and make sure you will not be disturbed for at least 30 minutes. Earplugs and a sleep mask may help if the light is too bright or the location has too much ambient noise.

Take a deep breath and relax into the support of the towels at your neck and back. As each breath is let out try to relax more and more. Then begin to listen to your breath as it moves in and out of your lungs. Think of becoming lighter with each breath, as if your consciousness of self was beginning to float. Let it become lighter and lighter until it floats out of the top of your head and into a black void. Inner space is not cold and airless, it is warm and enclosing and you are free to float further and further into its welcoming embrace.

Ahead of you is a bright point of light. Mentally will it to come closer and as it does so you see that it is a Pyramid with four sides built of coloured light each reflects one of the Briatic colours of the sphere of Malkuth. These are Citrine, Olive, Russet and Black. It comes closer and closer until it encloses you within itself. Light bursts in all directions and in that moment you become one with your own Inner Space. You have a physical body of Matter but here your consciousness exists at the level of Briah. Here you will build inner Places of Peace where nothing can touch or harm you and the silence is Absolute. You become aware of four great windows each one offering a different mental canvas on which to project your thoughts.

Concentrate on the first one. At first it shows the symbol of a Double Cube, then this dissolves into a star-filled void in which you see galaxies, suns, stars, novas and clouds of stellar dust floating in the void. As you fix your attention on one star, or galaxy it is magnified and fills the whole of your vision so you can examine it in detail. Choose what you wish to look at and you will find that even the furthest star is available to you.

Every star or galaxy projects a different colour and a different musical note but each person will see a different colour or hear a different note because we are individuals. It is part of your learning process to discover what colour and what musical note that star or galaxy shows to you. You can look into the heart of a galaxy and search out each planet in turn.

Most are barren, scorched, and arid, but a few are green and fertile. Some have seas but not all are of water, some are liquids you have no name for, if you find a star, planet or sun, or even a small moon that seems worthy of attention try to memorise the main areas to record in your diary.

Now look out through the second Face and see the symbol of an Equal Armed Cross. This dissolves into colours of every shade dark and light. They move and mix and slide over and through each other creating patterns and shapes, spirals, and interlaced patterns of intricate beauty. Sometimes they stop, frozen in mid change and you can magnify them and look into the heart of the particles that form their existence. You can distinguish the various degrees of heat that each colour commands and even feel it if you wish.

The three primary colours that your human eyes can see in Malkuth are here extended far beyond that range. You have no names to give to them, nor should you try to do so. You will only be able to see and experience them in this time and space.

Until this moment you have only seen, but now you can will yourself to hear as well. Sound bursts upon you like a choir of a million voices. Every minute shade of colour becomes a pure note, a thousand more than the human ear can know. You try to hold on to the experience knowing that this must be what it is like to hear the archangels sing the Gloria before the Throne of the Ultimate I AM. Let the sound and colour fade slowly into a silence and a darkness that is almost a blessing.

The third Face shows the symbol of a Magic Circle and within its circumference you see the forms and faces of all who have touched your life in this incarnation. You may or may not be able to remember their names but every face you have seen will be there, and not only faces, but places, and objects. Pets and toys once loved and lost, books you once read and remember but a few lines. Voices that used to teach you in primary school, the first Christmas tree you saw ablaze with lights. The moment you first saw a shooting star, or focussed on your mother's face. All these are part of the Briatic world of thought. Every life is a mosaic of colour, sound and form from the first moment of that life and will be remembered in retrospect at its ending. Select those you wish to see again, recall the forms and faces that you may have forgotten but that once helped to mould your character.

Now the last face shows its secrets. The symbol here is The Triangle of Evocation. Within it appears a labyrinth. It curves and swirls and doubles back and forth on itself time and again. At the entrance stands a facsimile of yourself. This labyrinth represents your life so far and the part still to come is dark and cannot be seen yet. But as you watch the figure begins its journey. As it comes to each life changing point it pauses and that particular event becomes available to you as a vignette allowing you to see what happened and how it affected the next part of your life. It will not allow you to change anything, but it will help you to understand its significance.

By seeing where the main important events took place you may be able to predict what and where the next one will occur since the labyrinth shows the pattern as a whole. But you will NOT be able to see further than the present moment. Don't worry if you are not able to get very much the first time. This whole course of instruction takes on average; two to three complete runs before it all snaps into place.

There is a moment of silence and darkness as your self-consciousness returns to the point where you first floated free of the head chakra. Sink down into the weight of the body and begin to become aware of your limbs, and the feel of the chair beneath you. Let full awareness come slowly and when you feel fully awake… open your eyes. The first time of working at this level can be disorienting and can take some getting used to. You are advised to take a hot drink and eat a small snack to help you settle back into the everyday world.

The next journey will take you into the highest of the four worlds so rest for a full 48 hours before undertaking it, more if you feel the need. These journeys are not to be hurried, but taken slowly and with care, paying attention to detail and allowing time for each one to be assimilated and recorded before going on.

Malkuth in Atziluth

As one gets higher on the Middle Pillar there is less and less that can actually be said, taught, or experienced about it. The reason is mainly because we have no words that can accurately describe the physical, astral, mental or spiritual emotions that it often brings about. What can one say about Malkuth in Atziluth? The nearest explanation I can offer is that it is The Realm of Human Ecstasy. Note that I use the words **human ecstasy.** Each level of Atziluth on the Middle Pillar spheres will bring about a similar state but on increasingly higher levels. The important thing about this level is to remember that ecstasy of this kind cannot be induced, it happens spontaneously.

Before people begin pointing it out... I have not forgotten about the use of drugs. I do not advocate the use of drugs, have never personally used drugs to bring about an altered state, and do not consider them needful in this context. I accept there are shamanistic groups, traditions, and sects that do use them to achieve similar results and that this is a living part of their culture. In the Traditional Western Mysteries this is not so and only the natural occurrence of the ecstatic state is acceptable. This lies within the capabilities of every human being to a greater or lesser degree and the use of artificial means is discouraged by all responsible schools.

We all have moments of ecstasy on a smaller scale. Holding a much wanted child for the first time, one's first real love affair, seeing Mount Everest for real, not a photograph. Simultaneous orgasm with a beloved partner. Such seemingly small moments in time can bring about the sudden lifting of consciousness to a point where just breathing is difficult and this constitutes a point of ecstasy.

There was a time before the world became so small, when there were still places to be discovered when moments of sheer wonder were more common. When the first western explorer looked on the immensity of the Pacific for the first time, when Hillary and Tenzing stood on the summit of Everest, when the first heart transplant was successful and Neil Armstrong placed his foot on the moon. These were moments when collectively humanity held its breath and touched a point of ecstasy.

The very word itself means different things to different people and because of our individual natures we will react accordingly. We must always take into account that the human mind is solipsistic, it exists alone like a hermit within the cave of the skull. Though we can and do take in and contemplate the ideas, thoughts and concepts of other human beings, they will always be coloured by the emotional, mental and spiritual state of our personal outlook.

The point of ecstasy when it involves another human being is the closest we can get to a "mind meld", (to use a *Star Trek* phrase). It is a moment of feeling, or emotional joining, but not a complete knowingness of everything in that other person's mind. Individuality is both a gift and a drawback. We can reach incredible heights of personal at-one-ness as an individual, but we can never share it completely with others. Looked at in another way, this is a mercy, for to be able to share another mind with all its hidden pains and fears, joys and hopes would be intolerable. Increase that by the amount of people in the world and humanity would be driven insane. Telepathy must, at least for the foreseeable future remain unobtainable for our sanity's sake.

23

However, in and at the level of Atziluth we enter a dimension where for brief moments in this space/time continuum it is possible for certain human beings to become one with their Creative source. This is certainly not possible for everyone. It would appear that on rare occasions, some men and women are born with the ability to lift themselves, or, to be lifted mentally to a level of consciousness so high they touch the Infinite. On even rarer occasions, perhaps once in several thousand years, this may even result in a bodily transformation, as with the stories of Enoch, Elijah, Jesus of Nazareth, and Mary. At this point we may also take into account those moments when very ordinary people vanish into thin air, as has been reported on occasion.

For those rare human beings who do achieve a spiritual Atziluth state whilst still in a physical state of Assiah it invariably damages the human body. Every saint who has done so has suffered a deterioration of some kind. If we look at Teresa of Avila, St John of the Cross, Bernadette of Lourdes, St Francis of Assisi we see someone who lives with physical and often mental pain and invariably such lives are shortened.

Why does this seem to occur most often to those living under a strict religious regime? Most often because their lives are disciplined and there are long periods of silence interspersed with prayer and introspection. The whole being is directed towards the inner universe instead of the outer. The outer world fades and becomes far less important. There is no need to seek employment in order to live. Stress, both mental and physical, is lower and the search for a personal understanding of the Source of Creation is always at the forefront of their daily lives.

As life has become more convoluted, more technological, and more demanding there is less and less time to seek out the higher worlds and discover their secrets. But even a few moments of personal introspection set aside on a daily basis can bring results of a high level.

Malkuth in Atziluth – Working

The safest way to touch the lower levels of Malkuth in Atziluth is by stripping away the levels of each stage and leaving them to be re- accessed on your return. Begin by arranging for at least an hour of undisturbed time, this will mean no mobiles, no landlines, no voices, no knocks on the door and as little extraneous noise as possible. This is vital as any disturbance can react on your finer senses. You will be working on a higher level than before and this must be taken into account.

Choose a chair with a firm supportive back, with another support beneath your feet. You should be able to relax enough to be comfortable, but not so much that you will fall asleep. Place a thermos with a hot drink close by, and a few biscuits (cookies). You will need to eat and drink something to help you close down, but do not do the working on a full stomach.

A dim light is preferable to darkness, drawn curtains with a small golden candle to one side is ideal. Gold is the Atziluthic colour of Malkuth. Prepare for your journey by sitting quietly for a few minutes and let your mind grow still. Begin to breathe slowly and more deeply than usual, follow the action of your breathing until you can feel your heartbeat slow down. Relax more deeply with each outward breath then begin to build in the inner eye an image of the wall opposite your chair. Create within you the sensation of your body getting lighter and lighter then imagine getting up and walking towards the wall. When you get there look back at your body. Contemplate it for a minute or so then turn and walk through the wall.

You are standing on the flat featureless plain of the Astral. Call up a scene of a high mountain range, like the Alps, or the Andes, or Himalayas. When it is all clear and stable, will yourself to the highest peak. There on the summit is a huge carved chair with a high back and a carved footstool to help you up. Wrap yourself in a thick golden cloak with a hood and sit in the chair. It will face in any direction you choose. You are now in Malkuth in Yetzirah but not for long. Look around you and you will find your sense of sight is magnified far beyond the usual. You can see for hundreds of miles in any direction. Take a few moments to try out this new sensation. Then look up.

Far above you lies a star filled void with one radiant star just above you. Mentally reach out to that star and allow yourself to be drawn upwards and outwards. Look down and see your astral body sitting in the Chair of Vision and note its position. It will remain there until you return. The star encloses you within itself, there is a moment of intense light then you are floating in a world of colour and sound. Very gently try to look down at yourself. Do it gently because there is nothing there. You are in the world of Briah, a mental level where form has no place, only vibration. Mentally sound your name and before you will appear a pattern of colours that is approximate to the form of your name, also a vibration of sound that is the pattern of your physical self. Just sound and colour that is what you are now in Briah. Keep the pattern and the sound before you, to do this keep repeating your name mentally. The pattern and the sound become stronger and louder until you are caught up in its vibration and drawn into the heart of your own primal pattern. That pattern will remain where it is until you reclaim it on your return.

You find yourself caught up in a spiral of light that winds its way up until it vanishes into the heart of a blazing sun bigger than anything you can imagine. You are just an infinitesimal point of light among billions, all making your way back into the Source of all Creation. All around you there is a vibration that becomes a cascade of sound. It is as if the universe, and every life form within it, has joined in a hymn of praise and thanksgiving for the Life it enjoys. Here and there are bigger and more brilliant points of light who seem to be guiding the smaller ones. As one of them passes you send out a thought.

"What are you? Why are you different from all these other forms of light?"

The light pauses and from it comes a tendril of radiance that touches, caresses, holds you and comforts you.

"These others are The Ashim, the Souls of Fire and the angelic choir of Malkuth. I am Sandalphon the Archangel of Malkuth and a Servant of the Most High. I guide those whose time has come to return to the Source. I know that you are of the world of Manifestation and so you come under my protection. But what are you doing here? Your time to return to the Great Source is not now."

You explain that you are a Seeker of Knowledge and Sandalphon enfolds you within its greater light and takes you closer to the great pulsating centre. From here you can dimly sense the power of the Primal Creator as it spins in an eternal dance, keeping everything, every particle of its "family" within its orbit. Sandalphon speaks:

"There is the Great Source from which we all spring. But it is not time for you to enter and be re-made. But I can and will ask a blessing for you."

It sends out a brilliant pulse of light towards the Centre, and for a smallest space of No Time everything stops. Then, from the Source comes a wave of love that touches you in the deepest part of your Being.

"Child of my Light, I bless you to the amount you are, at this moment, able to receive, when it is time... I will remember you."

The great spiral begins to move once more and the Guide takes you back to the point where you entered this level. The darkness encloses you and you find yourself back before the pulsing pattern of sound and colour that you are at this level. The blessing shines like a jewel in your heart centre and you can feel its warmth as you allow yourself to be drawn back towards the astral level.

There below you is your astral form in the Chair of Vision. You flow into it and draw in a breath, sit up and look around you. You focus on your physical body on the next level down and see it sitting in the chair, the tea light almost burnt out. You feel the call of the physical world and follow it down into the room from which you began this journey. You move through the wall and go to stand before your body. Pass to it the blessing you received from the Source and let it fill the heart centre. Then let your consciousness flow into it. Slowly become aware of the weight of the body and the room around you, begin to take deeper breaths and feel the air filling your lungs. Open your eyes and take in your surroundings. Rest for a few minutes, then take something to eat and drink, adjust to the world of Malkuth and share with it the blessing of the Source.

This completes the teachings of Malkuth in the Four Levels. The next set of journeys will take you through Yesod the Sphere of Dreams and Desires in the four worlds. Until then re-read your notes and try to find deeper realisations in them.

CHAPTER TWO

THE SPHERE OF YESOD

The Sphere of Dreams, Magic and Imagination

This is the second Sphere of the Royal Road and one of the most important. In some ways it links up with Daath the Penultimate Sphere of the Middle Pillar. It holds mysteries that need to be unfolded one by one and with great care. The word SUD means Mystery in Hebrew. Humanity has been given some incredible gifts, gifts that other species on this planet do not share. We can dream with purpose, some of the other animal species can dream but not with the clarity and depth that a human being can do. We can laugh and make others laugh, we can create whole scenarios inside our heads and exist within them; we can plan ahead and travel backwards and forwards in time through the medium of memory. Such gifts set us apart from other life forms.

The human brain is a miracle of engineering. It can hold a universe within itself and in the Sphere of Yesod we enter a virtually limitless landscape of imagery that belongs to us alone. It is a universe in which the human mind is both the creator and the created. The human brain contains billions of neurons, but, and this is a scientific fact, there are more connections between those brain neurons than there are atoms in the universe. If that does not make you pause and think, nothing will, and all this potential is yours to use, train, and develop. Add to this information the fact that the Vision associated with Yesod is called The Machinery of the Universe and you can begin to understand the importance of this sphere.

The brain uses physical sensations, visual memory, perception, and of course emotions to create an internal and solipsistic world in which the personal "I AM" or MIND is the sole occupant. It is this internal world that we are now preparing to experience. In Qabalistic terms it is known as Yetzirah, the natural world of Yesod. However Yesod itself also has a presence in Assiah the level of Malkuth, as indeed do all the spheres.

All the journeys are solitary in the sense that only the personal consciousness of the Self exists within the inner universe, it can only be shared with another person through words, writings, ideas and concepts; it cannot be shared in actuality, for only you exist within your personal world.

Dreams and imagined worlds are the product of a liaison between the mind and its memories and the stored knowledge and visual powers of the brain. We NEED to dream in order to keep sane. It is in the state of sleep and dreams that we process all the emotions, frustrations, joys and feelings that we experience in the outside world, and record them as memories. Such memories help us to learn how to cope with life and its lessons. "To sleep, perchance to dream", the poet told us and it is in those dreams that we can find the power of Yesod.

Yesod in Assiah

This is where we plan our hopes and desires and dream of the future we hope to have. Here we cherish our ambitions and, if we are lucky, see them come to fruition. In one sense this is where we set the course of our lives right from the beginning. The influences that surround us in our early years set patterns that, for the most part, we adhere to for the rest of our lives. A few are born with an indomitable will that can and will transcend difficulties posed by circumstances of birth and environment. Others will drift with the sea current of the life they were born into and never make it to the shore of attainment. A lot will depend on the way they look at life and the influence of the people around them.

Some are born fighters, they dream, plan, and believe in their ability to break through the barriers of birth circumstances. Boys have left school at fourteen and become millionaires without the benefit of a university education. Girls who were mothers at fourteen and fifteen have gone on to become teachers, doctors and owners of their own businesses and raised their families with love and success. Early poverty, deprivation, and uncaring parentage can and do leave lifelong mental and sometimes physical scars, but they can be overcome. There are three things going for you and three against you let's take the latter section first.

1.   **Parents, guardians, or those in authority over you.** If one's parents or foster parents are alcoholics, drug users, or abusers, a young life can become total misery. In some instances even the social workers are either uncaring and look upon their work simply as a pay check, or their hands are tied by bureaucratic red tape.

2.   **Peer pressure.** When surrounded by those of your own age and in the same situation as yourself it is all too easy to go with the majority and so escape the bullying and the threats that inevitably come when one tries to opt out of the "gang" mentality.

3.   **Apathy:** the inability to see any hope in one's situation.

The three things that are plus points are:

1.   Parents or a parent or a teacher who will encourage and support you.

2.   An inner strength and belief in your ability to fight against your present surroundings and those who try to drag you down.

3.   The ability to DREAM for the future. Note I say

FOR and not OF the future. The future is fluid and cannot be easily contained within a definite form, but it can be motivated and given positive directions. But in the end it all comes down to one's own inner strength of will and self-discipline. Both of which are hard to come by when the world seems to set its face against you. This feeling of helplessness can persist into adulthood and often leads to a life being allowed to drift without aim, hope or ideals.

Yesod in Assiah can offer a signpost leading to the way out of this apathy. The law of the universe is that everything seeks to descend from the highest to the lowest level. In other words intelligent life desires to experience manifestation; this applies to things spiritual as well. What we perceive as the Highest has to descend through a series of Portals as it gains mass. I AM moves from the Spiritual to the Mental then to the Astral and on to the Manifested World.

Yesod acts as a container, a vessel or Chalice where Spiritual matter, reinforced by its transit through the mental level pauses and awaits a form into which it can pour itself. When such a form is provided only then can it become a REALITY. As the prime level of the dream world Yesod holds the patterns of all our future hopes, fears, desires and needs but not only yours and mine, it holds ALL the patterns of everything that has been thought about, built, created or formed since this world began. Yesod is not called The Treasure House of Images for nothing.

The energy of thought is fluid; it can take the form of anything it is poured into. This is why we used thought-forms, dreams and our gift of imagination to create the God-forms of the ancient past and our hopes and desires for the future. We all play the game of… "what if I could have… could be… could do…?" This is natural, we all seek to be more than we are, and this is what was intended to be our progress towards the light.

Energy, thought, emotion and desire are the four cornerstones of existence. With these we can build whatever we want on the astral level. However in order to manifest it we need one more thing. WILL. Without the will to bring it into real time it will always remain a dream. Remember this. "Many people dream of great things, a few wake up and MAKE THEM COME TRUE". Nothing comes free... everything has its price and that price usually means you have to get off your butt and help things along. All too often this is enough to deter your dream becoming a reality. Be prepared to pay a price in energy: physical, mental or emotional.

Yesod in Assiah – Working

As before and as with all pathworkings select a time and place where you will not be disturbed for at least 20 to 30 minutes. Once the location, intent, and focal point of the working are secure the time can be shortened by shifting your mental location directly to the chosen point of view and proceeding with the working. However until you are confident doing this, continue with the preparations as given.

Choose a firm backed chair in a dimly lit room and, because one of the symbols of this sphere is Perfume, choose to burn a simple lavender incense and prepare to relax. Pay attention to your shoulders, often one of the most tense areas of the body. As you begin to breathe slowly in and out relaxing on each out breath until you feel yourself ready to begin the working. The intent here in Yesod of Assiah is simple you are going to attempt to manifest a ten dollar/ten pound sterling note! Why JUST ten dollars? Because your human mind can actually believe in that amount appearing in your life... whereas it would have great difficulty in imagining a million dollars doing the same thing. Starting small is always a good idea.

Withdraw into the quiet darkness of the mind and imagine yourself sitting in the darkness of an empty cinema. You are dressed in the Colour of Yesod at this level which is a robe of citrine flecked with blue. The curtains sweep back and you face a black screen. Leave your seat and approach the screen. Think of the liquid "wormhole" we see when we watch an episode of *Stargate* only this is black. Walk through the screen and into a tower room in an ancient castle. It is full of strange objects, crystal balls, bubbling glass bottles in which colours swirl and mix and from where occasionally, weirdly shaped faces peer out. Huge leather bound books lie everywhere in profusion, some lie open to show symbols and writings you cannot understand. Amid all this clutter a small man with a long white beard, dressed in a dark blue robe covered with astrological symbols and wearing a tall pointed hat is busy stirring a large cauldron poised over a single candle flame with a wooden spoon.

He lifts the spoon and sniffs, then takes a cautious taste, after a second or two of lip smacking he adds a small clove of garlic to the mixture and stirs again. Then he looks up at you and smiles. "Vegetable and wild mushroom soup," he explains, "would you like a bowl?" You may accept or not as you please. Merlin sweeps a pile of books off a sagging armchair and invites you to sit down.

A little bemused by your surroundings you do so, still looking around you at the confusion of furnishings, books, and chemical paraphernalia. Some of it looks far too modern to be believable in this setting. Merlin clears another space and sits opposite you with a bowl of soup and a white napkin tucked into his robe.

"I expect you are wondering why this particular location has been chosen." He pauses and wipes his beard with the napkin, "Well, you see it all has to do with psychology. Your subconscious associates Magic with Merlin and places that look like this." He waves his spoon around at cluttered room. "The

34

human mind has been conditioned for centuries to think of Magic as being the stuff of which Fairy Tales are made. So something like this helps you to believe in the unbelievable. Besides, humour relaxes you and helps me… I'm your subconscious mind by the way… to create an inner reality where you can feel comfortable. Too much intellectuality makes it difficult for the conscious mind to use the creative power all humans have." He pauses to finish off the soup.

"Now as I understand it you are here to manifest a ten pound note, or ten dollars as the case may be. I am fairly certain you have already decided in your conscious mind to ask for, or to manifest, much more than that." He pauses and looks at you searchingly. "Yes, I thought so. However the sum of ten has already been set cosmically for this time and cannot be changed. You see if you try to manifest more before you are sure of being able to manifest a smaller amount you risk being disappointed and put off the whole idea. It is easier to imagine making a ten pound note than to imagine making a hundred." He waves a hand and a small table appears in front of you set with a tea or coffee pot (according to your preference) and two mugs along with cream and sugar.

"You will also have been told that nothing comes free… including money. There are four ways to obtain ten pounds/dollars. You can earn it, you can find it, you can receive it as a gift, or it can be repaid as a debt. Between them these four ways encompass every possible way to get your hands on that money. You see 'magic' is an energy that is exchanged with, by, and for other energies. It does not matter how it is exchanged. 'Money' is simply another energy that is exchanged with, by, and for other energies and the **manner** in which one comes by it does not matter.

"For instance you can earn it by doing some extra work… simple, easy, but predictable. You can find it… this means going out and actually looking for it on the highways and byways, very inefficient. As a gift, this can mean someone giving it to you as a birthday/Christmas gift or even getting a coupon in the post or in a magazine for a credit to that amount, or a credit note for something you have returned. You may have loaned money to someone in the past and they decide now is the time to repay it, or you can decide to sell some of your books, or an unwanted gift, or trade something for something else worth that amount.

"It does **not** mean you will suddenly find the money under your pillow or that it will come in a shower of gold from the ceiling. It can be as simple as finding a forgotten note in an old coat or purse. Magic will always find the most direct or convenient way (in your space/time) to manifest the required object. Your task is to prepare yourself to receive the money, to expect it, to plan for it and… **most importantly to pass it on**. To hold on to it means you create a bottleneck that will prevent more money from flowing through it. So tithe a bit, spend a bit and save a little to act as a seed for more.

"Tithing is an ancient way of saying thank you to the 'gods'. They do like to be acknowledged so pass on one pound/dollar to a charity box, buy something for 1 or 2 pounds/dollars for yourself, and put the rest in a piggy bank on your desk as 'seed'. One final piece of advice, thank the universe for providing it and ask for another ten when the opportunity presents itself. This is most important as the request then goes into the world memory and becomes an on-going order form.

"Do not allow yourself to be tempted into asking for very large amounts by using this method, this is just to encourage your belief in being able to do it. Large amounts need a plan and a commitment to that plan and the offer of being willing to work for its success. All Magic works by using universal laws to supply the demand. 'Disney' magic is just… fantasy. To receive you must learn to give. Now, I want you to build this scenario in your imagination. Compose a short letter to the universe along these lines.

"Dear universe, I am in need of ten pounds/dollars (do NOT use the word want) I realise I must give something in exchange to keep the balance and this I am willing to do and I will tithe in the ancient way. I place a time lock of two weeks on this request. As I will so mote it be. A blessing on those who bring this to pass'.

"Place this in a mental envelope and seal it then, again mentally, summon an angelic messenger and ask it to deliver the message to The Universe at the Atziluthic level of creation. The angels of Yesod are called The Cherubim (pronounce it as Kerubim). As this will be instantaneous you can then proceed to the next stage and visualise the required sterling/dollar bill (in as much detail as you can) being put into an envelope and sent, via the same messenger back down to the Yetziratic level, where the angel will keep hold of it until the time comes for it to manifest.

"This is where the cogs and wheels of circumstance will start to create the way in which it will manifest. From this moment you can decide what you are going to do to deserve it. Start looking through old coats, keep an eye on the pavements and sidewalks for loose money, see if there is something you can sell, or work you can do. Make yourself open to receiving what is already on its way to you. Within twice seven days it should be yours. Remember 90% of it relies on your ability to believe in your own inner divine power to create the pathway from the level of Atziluth to Assiah via Yesod.

"Good Luck. Now return to your own level and await the results." Merlin dismisses you with a wave of his hand and returns to his own work. You find yourself back in the empty cinema. Take a deep breath and as you let it out return to your own physical level.

Yesod in Yetzirah

Here Yesod is in its own level of reality, that of dreams, desire, fulfilment, fantasy and thought-forms, hence one of its many titles The Treasure House of Images. It is also the level of what we might describe as The Spiritual Theatre for it is here that we can act out our desires no matter how strange or bizarre in the absolute privacy of the human mind.

Another of Yesod's titles is that of The Machinery of the Universe. This can apply to the outer universe at large in which we exist and move and live out our brief span of life or the inner, intensely personal universe inside our heads. We are in point of fact multi-dimensional beings, for we have the ability to experience a full awareness in both of these universes.

As the Treasure House, Yesod in Yetzirah holds the pattern and the memory of every idea, desire, dream, or fantasy we have ever had. As the Machinery of the Universe it holds the pattern and memory of everything that has taken place on this planet since its inception. As that which is named the Sphere of Foundation it houses the creative ability of both the Creator and the Created. So it is the most magical of all spheres.

The importance of this Sphere on all its levels is indicated by its position, for if you fold the Tree of Life in half you will find Yesod occupies the space of Daath, the mysterious sphere that has a dual existence of Being and Not Being a part of the whole. It is here in Yetzirah that we find the Angelic Choir of the Cherubim who are also called "The Builders". This is highly significant as Yesod is the Sphere of the Prototype, the detailed Plan of all that descends from Kether with the aim of manifesting in Malkuth. All such "plans" MUST pass through Yesod before they become a reality in our world.

Before manifestation there has to be the plan of form, before the plan of form there has to be an idea, before the idea there has to be the Desire to Become. Yetzirah is the penul-

38

timate stage before the final descent into the world of reality therefore it is the place of dreams, hopes, and pre- destiny. But not all dreams and fantasies come true or indeed are meant to come true.

As I have already pointed out human beings have the ability to exist and to experience existence on many levels. Our everyday world gives us complete reality, here we live, move and obey the laws that physical life demands. But we can also exist in the non-material world of Yetzirah which is a fluid world that can change in accordance with our will and desire. We can also reach with some training, the mental world of ideas. Both the committed past and the changeable future are available to us as what has been and what might be possible.

Even a prototype plan can be changed at the last minute so the level of Yetzirah should be seen as the point of no return. A level where a decision must be made and committed to so what has been created can become reality and in doing so, it will become part of the past. The present as a point in time barely exists, like dark matter it comes and goes without our being aware of it in our lives. As soon as it "becomes" it passes into the "has been". Yesod in Yetzirah is the only place where the present can be held in a constant state of "becoming".

This is also the level where lucid dreaming occurs. Lucid dreams are more common than was once thought and happens when one part of the conscious mind awakens within the dream state. One becomes aware that one is dreaming and to an extent can then take some control of the actual dream itself. With practice the lucid state can be induced. The most common realisation that one is dreaming lucidly is to hear someone calling you name. You seem to wake up and get out of bed but when you try to turn on the light your hand goes through the switch. If this happens, you have entered a lucid dream.

Another area of the Yetzirah level is concerned with out of the body experiences and what is known as the hypnagogic state. Both work in a similar way to lucid dreaming and can bring about visionary experiences as well as nightmares. Such experiences were probably the source of the tales of Succubi and Incubi where sexual dreams become distorted and alarming especially to those of a sensitive nature. Such images occur as one begins to slide into sleep, or, to emerge from a deep sleep. It is a time when we are most likely to see visions, forms, shapes, or experience astral imagery. However dreaming is necessary to mental health for it allows the brain to sort out problems, fears, anxieties we have incurred during the day. The advice to "sleep on a problem" is well founded. But it is also a time when we can enact the desires we keep hidden even from ourselves.

Whether we indulge in daydreams or night dreams or a mixture of both, they evolved as a way of clearing the brain of unwanted odds and ends and/or indulging in what the conscious mind regards as something to keep hidden from prying eyes, or things we may feel ashamed of thinking, doing, or experiencing in real life. However the mind and the brain working together know what is best for us and dreams are often their way of keeping us sane and reasonably healthy. If your dreams are of a sexual nature it is because that is what you need to look at in your life. It may be a way of siphoning off tension or calling attention to a lack on the everyday level. Either way it pays to keep a dream diary and take note of what comes up in them. Think of it as self-psychology!

This leads us into the pathworking for Yesod in Yetzirah and it is time to loosen up the inhibitions. Nowhere else can you indulge yourself so completely as in a daydream. As I have told you, on this level and within the universe of the mind there is no one else but you. There is no one to tell you it is unladylike, self-indulgent, or distasteful. This is your world and you can people it with who and what you like... As long as you realise that they will all be simulacrums of yourself in disguise. This

40

also applies to those times when you summon someone from the past to talk with or discuss a problem, such as a God-Form or a philosopher, etc. The form will be of your own making and the information will come either from your own sub-conscious mind advising you or, more rarely from a Being on another level via your sub-conscious. Even more rarely it can occasionally be a direct communication.

Every human being has desires, most will never come true, a few will, but here, in Yesod in Yetzirah, you can have what you desire for a while. You may find that it is not as good as you thought it would be. You may find living an idle life is boring even in a dream world. Even here in a dimension where you can create anything you want you can learn things about yourself. You can live events at first hand and what you thought might be something great could turn out to be not as good as you had hoped. On the other hand as long as you understand that all this is taking place inside your personal universe you can obtain experience without the side effects you would get in real life.

Do you have a favourite book, an adventure story, a thriller, or a romance? You can become the hero or heroine and experience the story from within the pages as it were; you can even change the story to suit yourself if you do not like the ending.

Everything on the Astral Level is in a potential state halfway between being and not being and therefore it can be changed at will. Once you enter this level of Yesod you are in the position of being able to create your own environment, your own persona and your own "daydream". Nothing is impossible for you to imagine, if you can visualise it, you can create it in Yetzirah. This is your private world. However there are rules and there are dangers.

Rule one. Never interact **emotionally** with the simulacrum of a living Being. By creating such a link you may interfere with that person's life path. It happens to Pop Stars and Film

Celebrities. Fans imagine themselves in an emotional contact with them and because emotion is the most powerful psychic tool in our make-up, it can and often does cause a rift between the real person and anyone they are connected to. This kind of interplay is the basis of what we know as a "curse". The emotion used to play out a daydream is often either love or hate… sexual or combative and like a heat seeking projectile it will seek out its object of intent and fasten on to it with predictable results.

Rule two. Get it into your head that at this level emotion is a two edged sword. Desire, emotion, visualisation, and intent are the four corners of ritual and if misused or overused such a ritual can take on a purpose of its own and may well cut loose from its creator and cause damage to both you and the object of desire.

Danger. Do NOT over indulge in daydreams and fantasies they can become as addictive as any hallucinogenic drug. They can cause an energy leak that eats through the Etheric and the Auric layers surrounding our physical bodies and lead to physical illness, debilitation and even some forms of disease such as Diabetes, something that is very common among occultists.

Danger. Too much reliance on day dreaming can lessen your effectiveness on the physical plane and make you unable to deal with the everyday world. It can turn you into a dreamer who never completes anything you begin. Dream by all means, then wake up and start working on making the dream come true.

Yesod in Yetzirah – Working

As usual make sure you will not be disturbed during your session by people, mobiles, or telephones. Choose a comfortable chair with a supportive back in a dimly lit room. Spend a few minutes breathing deeply and slowly and filling the lungs with each breath. Slow down the heartbeat and make sure the shoulders are relaxed with the hands resting lightly on your lap. Close your eyes and build up the inner image of a starry night with a thin crescent moon. You are wearing a robe of deep purple, the colour of this level of Yesod and silver sandals, also one of the symbols of Yesod. When this is as clear as you can make it create a spiral pathway between you and the New Moon. It is translucent but solid enough to take your ethereal weight as you climb up towards the crescent.

As you get nearer you see that the crescent is actually opening up to become a doorway into another level of consciousness. Beyond it there are no stars, just blackness. Step over into this new dimension and feel it envelop you and draw you onward, upward and inward. There is a moment of dis-orientation, then open your inner eyes. You are standing before a full-length mirror hanging in space. You see yourself in your physical form. If you wish to change how you look you in this dimension you can do it now. Ask yourself what you want to change, height, weight, colouring, gender, race, everything is open to you.

With your newly created persona you can play the part of a celebrity on the red carpet at a premiere, or act out a scene from your favourite movie. You can become royalty. You can even take on the form and face of a past historical figure and re-live moments of History.

Having done that you can now decide what kind of environment you want to establish in your dream world. Do you want a simple life or one of luxury, life as a celebrity or as an academic, would you like a medieval castle or a penthouse? Here you have the ability to create what you desire and what is more, to create the company you need to fill this world. If you do not like what you build you can dissolve it and try again. Here your wishes and your desires are uppermost. In fact, you can have all this in the same way that you can have it in the cyber world of *Second Life,* but without any cost, or learning how to control your person via a computer. The animation is much better as well! While you are still thinking it over let me provide you with an example. When in doubt turn to mythology.

Gentlemen how do you feel about becoming a God?

Since we have a whole pantheon to choose from we can look for the best as it does not matter if you are fifty and bald or in your twenties with a six pack. So let's go for Apollo. Apollo is the Sun God of ancient Greece. Supposedly the most hand-some of them all; tall, athletic, golden haired and drives the chariot of the Sun across the sky each day. His love affairs like those of his father Zeus are numerous and include both sexes. His resting place during the hours of night was located on the isle of Delos. After more than 2000 years it is still a place of pilgrimage and regarded as a Holy Place. The atmosphere is in-credible. So let us begin. Look into the mirror again and begin to change yourself.

Mid to late twenties, six foot, golden hair worn long to the shoulders, eyes blue/grey, clean shaven. Typical Greek athletic build, lean and sinewy. Arms in particular are muscular, guid-ing four lively horses across the world for the whole day needs strength. Clothed in a golden robe reaching to mid-thigh. Look on the web for pictures of statues to help you visualise the finer details. Once you have the reflection changed it is time to change yourself. Have the reflection turn round (you may have to touch up the visualisation on the back view) and then walk forward and into the form.

Pause and begin to make yourself familiar with your new body. Turn round and look into the mirror again. There will be a difference here, before you were looking into a mirror at a form you had built; now you must look into the mirror as if you were actually looking from behind the eyes of Apollo. SEE yourself as Apollo.

Now build in your mind the Hall of the Sun on the island of Delos (you do not have to do all this in one session) Imagine standing on the balcony looking East just before Dawn. Below you servants have opened the door and rolled out the Sun Chariot. It is made of gold, but magic has made it light enough to fly. Now the servants lead out the four fire horses and harness them to the chariot. They are beautiful, their coats gleam with a mixture of red and gold, their manes and tails are long and flowing and their hooves are shod with pure gold.

You fasten your cloak of golden silk and descend the stairway, waiting for you are twelve young women dressed in filmy white. They are the twelve hours of day and they accompany you on your daily journey. Another woman, even more beautiful stands before the Horses who are stamping impatiently and waiting to the moment of release. The young woman looks up at you and you nod your head. She runs lightly across the marble flooring and leaps into the air. At once the darkness begins to lift, for she is Aurora the Goddess of the Dawn. She is your herald and goes before you to awaken the sleeping world.

You mount the chariot and take up the reins the servants loose their hold on the bridles and stand back, you slap the reins against the horses' rumps and shout

pano kai pros ta empros

Onward and upward!

The horses lean into the harness and race forward to where the marble patio ends and falls away to the valley below. They surge into the air leaving a trail of light behind them and the dancing hours surround you though as each hour ends one of them will drop away. You urge the chariot onwards and up fill-

45

ing the sky with warmth and light. There is light and fire within and around you and you throw back your head and laugh with joy of life.

As you rise higher another figure appears beside you running yet keeping up with you easily. Hermes your half-brother comes to share your journey for a while. His winged sandals keep pace with the horses and those on his hat add extra fleetness. He laughs and throws his Herald's staff with its entwined serpents into the air and the tiny wings supporting the caduceus speed ahead of him. You trade brotherly insults back and forth and then with a wave of his hand Hermes snatches back his staff and puts on a burst of speed and departs on his Father's errand. You continue to rise to the zenith of the day looking down on the world below. Around you only six of the hours are left.

In the vault of Heaven you pause the horses for a brief moment to savour the feeling of being "The Sun God". You are at this moment "The Light of the World". Know your power, but know also that it is borrowed from the Primal Creator. Now take up the reins once more and begin your homeward journey, the arc you have travelled now turns downwards and back to your beloved Delos where a soft couch and a pair of loving arms await you, for even the Gods need love. Soon your sister Artemis will be harnessing her silver Moon Chariot with its milk white horses and, accompanied by the twelve Hours of the Night will be getting ready to take her turn at lighting the world.

You are pleasantly tired and as you look across to the western sky you see the Goddess of Night beginning to spread her black and grey cloak on the horizon. You gather your power and spread the colours of sunset and fling them like an artist using his paints across the canvas of the evening sky. In a riot of colour you slowly descend towards Delos, passing the Goddess of Night bowing gracefully to her and accepting her smile of recognition.

Ahead the servants are opening the doors of the stable, the horses will be cleaned, fed and watered and settled for the night. The chariot will be polished and made ready for tomorrow. You land softly and with care and step wearily from it to be welcomed with a cup of spiced wine and a kiss from the lips of your latest love. Ahead is a night of rest, love, and dreams. Stand on the balcony as you did this morning and look out into the night sky and see before you a full-length mirror. Reflected in it is your own true self, it turns presenting its back to you and you feel the pull of the physical world. Walk into the mirror and your physical self and you are back in your own time and space.

Female Pathworking

You can use Yesod in Yetzirah to re-enact any of the ancient myths, or you can devise your own scenarios. This is the play world of astral projection. Enjoy it. But now let us look towards the female side of things. Use the same method of entry into the required level of consciousness and look into the mirror.

Remember that the same rules apply; age, gender, race, do not matter here. We will follow the same path as with the male working and use a mythological setting. As you look into the mirror begin to change your reflection into that of the Greek Goddess of Love and Beauty, the wondrous Aphrodite. Let me emphasise once again your own age, colour, or gender do NOT matter. There is no reason whatsoever why Aphrodite cannot be African, Indian (either Hindi or First Nation), Caucasian or Asian. The same thing applies to transgender, what matters is that this is done with intent, with grace, and with an open heart.

Look at pictures of **The Birth of Venus** (Aphrodite) and get an idea of her stance, her gestures, and her surroundings. See the figure in the Mirror turn away from you, wait for a minute, focus your intent, and then walk into the mirror and into the Goddess-form. Sink into the womanly shape, feel the ultra-femininity flow through your veins. Stretch your arms over your head and feel the goddess within awaken to her full power. You ARE Aphrodite the Goddess of Love and Beauty. Aphrodite was born from the foam of the sea so we begin deep under the waves where all is blue and green with flashes of silver. You begin to rise up floating to the surface, you are newly born, innocent, fragile, unaware of who and what you are and will become.

As you near the surface the waves begin to foam and spin, the sun touches them with golden light to enhance your form; the four winds gather and combine to form a funnel of air, drawing down the fine mist of the clouds to become your voice. Birds offer their graceful flight and their song as their gift to the new-born Goddess. The Sea offers pearls for your skin, coral for your lips. A huge oyster shell floats to the surface and opens up to become your chariot, drawn on coloured strands of mermaids hair by white-breasted doves.

The Earth offers perfumes for your breath, flowers for your cheeks and breasts. You stand upon the shell and look around you wondering at the beauty of land and sea. The people of the deeps gather around you adoring your beauty and singing to welcome you to earth. Nearer and nearer to the land you come until before you is the soft sand of Paphos on the island of Cyprus. There to welcome you are the women of the island. They carry flowers for your hair, gold and silver to adorn your neck, wrists and ears, and gossamer linen to cover your nakedness. As yet you have no words so you smile and touch their smiling faces with your slender fingers.

There is the sound of rushing winds and a man stands before you. He is young and handsome and welcomes you with a smile; his eyes are bright and sparkling. On his feet are winged sandals and on his head a helmet also winged. In his hand he carries a golden rod around which wind two serpents one of silver and one of gold. At the top of the rod is a pine- cone with small wings outstretched on either side.

This is Hermes the son of Zeus and the messenger of the Gods. He is here to escort you to the Halls of Olympus where you will take your place among the immortals. Hermes steps forward and bends his head to kiss your lips, the first kiss you have known and with this kiss he gives you a voice and words. He also gives you a name, Aphrodite.

"Kalimera Aphrodite, Goddess of Love and Beauty I have come to conduct you to Olympus where the Gods have gathered to welcome you."

He steps forward and with great care lifts you into his arms. You can smell the male scent of him mixed with air, wind, salt, and sun warmed skin and feel the strength of his muscles. New emotions stir within you and you smile into his eyes and wind your arms about his neck. He lifts into the air holding you close against him and laughs mischievously.

"You may try your wiles on me young Goddess but better and higher fare than I will welcome you in Olympus. Best you wait until you see what others your beauty will enthral."

The journey is swift and soon you can see the snowy heights of Olympus and shiver at the thought of living there. But as you drop down you see there is another side to the mountain. A place of green meadows and flower filled gardens, pools of crystal water and stately marble halls where the Gods have their dwellings.

Hermes sets you down at the entrance to the largest Hall, the home of Zeus the Ruler of the Gods. Then he takes your hand and leads you into the hall. It is filled with beautiful people, men and women and Hermes names them as you pass. Each one inclines their head in welcome, though the women whisper behind their hands while the men look on you with hot, covetous eyes. As yet new in your power you lower your eyes shyly, grateful for the strong hand of Hermes.

"This is Athene, Goddess of wisdom and of war, She can be fierce but is also a good friend to have, but never touch her owl, it nips. This is Demeter, Goddess of the earth, a gentle soul. Here is Poseidon. God of the Oceans, brother to Zeus, and Thetis, his lady wife, and here is my half-brother Apollo who drives the Chariot of the Sun and his twin sister Artemis who is the Moon. You can trust both of them... well... almost.

"Pluto, Lord of the Underworld and his love Persephone. She is the daughter of Demeter by her brother Zeus and also my half-sister. Hephaestus, the Master Smith, son of Zeus and Hera, he makes the most exquisite jewellery. Ares here is the second son of Zeus and Hera, a bully and not very bright, but a nice enough boy. There are others you will meet later, Aurora, Dionysius, Pan, Hecate, but they are not often here." He pauses before two great golden thrones and bows.

"My lord Father Zeus, and my lady Stepmother Hera... may I present the oceans of the world's gift to Olympus, Aphrodite born from the foam to become the Goddess of Love and Beauty." He tugs on your hand to let you know to bow low before the King of the Gods and his Queen. Zeus rises and comes down from his throne to embrace you, his kiss is a little too intimate and Hera rises and sweeps him out of the way to bestow her own welcome.

"We welcome you to Olympus Aphrodite, you may take your place among us." She points to the last of the seats, far from the Thrones and by the door. But Zeus is having none of it... he takes your hand and seats you on a cushion at his feet.

"Hera my dear, it is far too draughty there, let her sit here between us, after all is it not fitting that Love itself should sit between the two who rule Olympus."

Hera scowls but grudgingly moves to one side. The silence is now broken and the feasting begins. The lesser gods serve the greater and Hebe, daughter of Hera, moves among the guests with a jug of ambrosia that never empties. Food follows and the nymphs dance. Apollo is persuaded to play the lyre and he and Hermes sing a song dedicated to Love and Beauty.

Hermes has elected himself your guardian and protector this night and stays close to whisper gossip and news about each of the gods as they move about the great hall. You are grateful for his company in this place where everything is new and a little frightening. Zeus and his son Hephaestus speak quietly together, often casting glances your way and you know they are talking about you. Hermes is summoned by Zeus and has to leave you, but Ares in his shining golden armour comes to take his place and you feel strangely happy when he is there. He is very big and rather clumsy and not as good a talker as Hermes, but he is kind and brings you food and wine and tells you silly jokes about the other gods and makes you laugh.

At last Hermes returns and tells you he will take you to your new Hall where all has been prepared for you. Servants with torches came to light the way and Ares kisses your hand and bids you to sleep well. You take your leave of Zeus and Hera and follow Hermes to a small but beautiful marble palace. Here a bath has been prepared and a couch covered with rare furs and silks. Hermes leaves you with your attendants promising to come for you the next day and show you around Olympus.

You bathe in the rose scented bath and allow your servants to array you in a soft linen shift then they bid you goodnight and leave. You go to look at yourself in the great bronze mirror. But as you look you see the Goddess change into your own physical self. It turns away and stands waiting. You pass through the mirror and into your own time and space. You wake in your own physical body and take time to adjust to being yourself again.

Yesod in Briah

The creative power of Yesod in Briah is a very mental one. This is the level at which World changing and life-enhancing inventions come into being. This is the birthplace of new ideas, books that make us think in new ways, where sculptures and pictures expressing the highest ideals of humankind are first formulated. The level at which the finest minds are imprinted by the power of the Primal Source flowing into them.

From this level came the idea that made Archimedes jump from his bath and run naked into the street shouting Eureka. This is the level at which Newton, Plato, Da Vinci Aristophanes, Hawking, Arthur Clarke, Marie Curie, Edison, and many others found themselves when reaching for new ways in which to think and understand the reality of the world about them. It is the level from where Shakespeare, Shelley, Keats, Tennyson, Longfellow, Poe and Whitman drew their immortal verse.

This level is the very crucible of thought, effort, despair, elation and genius. It often brings despair when the human brain cannot find the words to describe what they see or intuit. This is often how new words come into being. When the mind is forced into a situation where ordinary terminology does not suffice, the very pressure of the level itself forces us to invent new ways of communication.

This was the impulse behind the need to invent language, the desperate need to express feelings of emotions, anger and frustration elation and contentment and fear. Out of this came... WORDS. Sound symbols that conveyed how our ancestors felt at certain points in their all too brief lives. Until then there had only been grunts and gestures. But when one begins to THINK, words become necessary to convey the thoughts. Without speech nothing can be passed on to others, with it we can share ideas, concepts, images and emotions.

This level is also the level (as it is in all the spheres) of the archangelic world. In Yesod this means Gabriel and considering that we have been speaking about words, communication and speech in general who better than The Messenger of God to rule this sphere. Along with the whole concept of speech Gabriel rules the element of Water and is responsible for its well-being along with Nixsa the Elemental ruler of the element. The oceans of this planet teem with life and the sea is in effect our mother element. All life forms on this planet evolved from its watery womb. In mythology all goddesses with oceanic or water connections of any kind are considered to be a part of the Maternal Aspect.

It is this level of Yesod that has brought about an incredible surge of inventions in the last 100 years, more than at any other time in our planet's history. Even the least psychic of those among us can feel the tension building up towards a tremendous leap forward for the human race.

Colin Wilson, author of *The Outsider, Mysteries, The Occult,* and *Frankenstein's Castle* says... "It is past the time for mankind to take the next step... the two world wars have held us back, but now the time is near, and it will be the biggest step so far."

YES, but forwards... or backwards? OUT to the stars, or BACK into the dark ages? **The Machinery of the Universe** could grind to a halt if we are not careful. We are breeding ourselves out of existence and exterminating other species in our drive to accommodate our own species and this world cannot sustain much more. All the water available to us on this planet is here and now. There is no more water to be had anywhere. We cannot make more and what we do have is barely enough for the billions of life forms now crowding the world. Yesod as the Sphere of the element of Water is crucial to life on Earth yet we continue to pollute this, our most precious resource of all.

At the mental level thought takes many forms, not just words and images but colours, symbols, and sounds all of which are methods that convey thoughts. We use colours to explain feelings. We feel "blue" if we are sad, or describe ourselves as being "blue with cold", "red with anger", in a "brown study", "green with jealousy". "Yellow bellied" is used to describe cowardice.

At this level the colour of Yesodic power is Violet. Traditionally the wings and robes of Gabriel are white, silver and violet.

We use symbols in the same way as non-verbal instructions. An outstretched hand palm means STOP, but a crooked finger beckons us on. A clenched fist indicates anger, a finger can point out the way to go, or show us something to observe. We are told that a picture can convey a thousand words, and a picture or a symbol can convey a thought or a succession of thoughts or even a series of differing emotions. The great artists of past times have shown us this in their paintings.

I have often emphasised in my lectures and workshops the importance of observation, not just looking at something but observing it in depth. This skill is of great importance in this kind of work and study and we see it in action in Raphael's (1483-1520) painting *The School of Athens* (1510- 11).

This is a perfect example of observation. Its subject is "The Athenian School of Thought" and depicts a group of famous Greek philosophers gathered around Plato and Aristotle. Each figure is seen in a characteristic pose. Plato for instance points up towards the world of ideas while Aristotle points downwards to indicate the world of experience.

Raphael shows us the energy of physical and mental power by the grouping of his figures. Body and spirit, action and feeling, are balanced harmoniously, and each figure is painted with precision. The setting is classical and suited to the occasion. We see the philosophers of Ancient Greece gathered together with each one clearly depicting their particular topic or expertise. We see two of the ancient Gods influencing these great men. Minerva/Athena the goddess of wisdom occupies one niche and represents the style of rational thought, while Apollo/Helios the god of poetry and music stands opposite and oversees the inspirational style. The arc framing the painting draws the whole thing together. The groupings are random as they would be in such a gathering but the composition is full of energy and by close observation one can pick out each face and see how they interact with each other.

All too often we look at something and see it as a whole but go no further. Every painter of the renaissance was either an initiate of the mysteries or was aware of its influence. When they painted pictures such as this they did it with purpose and hid within it their own thoughts and ideas that would be obvious to those with like training. If we observed the world around us with the same attention to detail we would all be touched by genius.

Yesod in Briah – Working

Follow the usual instructions with regard to privacy, quietness and choice of chair. Begin by breathing and relaxing on each out breath paying particular attention to the shoulders where tension is most likely to occur.

Imagine yourself wearing a deep violet robe and silver sandals and standing at the entrance to a corridor painted in light colours. On each side are pictures of green fields, gardens of flowers, forests and woodlands. At the end of the corridor is a door through which you pass… into another corridor but here the colours are darker and the lights are dimmer. These paintings show moonlight on snowy roads, or seascapes with a lunar crescent above them, and one shows a solitary Hare sitting under a full moon and gazing up at it. When you get to the end of this corridor go through the door and emerge on the level of Yesod in Briah.

You stop on the threshold and look out over a vast empty sky filled with clouds. You hold on to the door feeling a little dizzy, but the feeling soon passes and you remember what you have learned about observation. You lean out as far as is safe and look around you. There is nothing but a blue sky and a warm sun.

A small cloud passes the doorway and pauses before you, you get the feeling it is looking at you, but you do nothing, so the cloud moves on. Another one comes along and does the same thing... But you don't move and the cloud passes. What should you do? A slightly larger cloud drifts up to the door and stops and then begins to change shape until it looks rather like a large bed. You wonder about this, and as you do the cloud passes on. Another appears stops, and changes its shape to look like a large and comfy looking armchair. You finally get the idea, you are being invited to take a ride and with a little jump you settle into the chair and it moves off.

As you float along you begin to wonder about the shape shifting clouds and decide to try an experiment... After all this is Briah, the level of Thought and Thought Forming. You decide to change the clouds shape to that of an old-fashioned claw footbath. It does and, much to your delight, you spend a few minutes changing your conveyance from one form to another.

You are reclining on a sofa and wondering where you are going when it occurs to you that on this level it is YOU who must create the destination. Then you notice the balloons. They are drifting along in twos, threes and small groups, all colours and even shapes and all have long ribbons attached to them. They also have words on them...

CREATIVE MOMENTS, PROBLEM SOLVING, DEALING WITH WORRIES, HEALTH, CREATING MONEY,

HAPPINESS, CONTENTMENT, MAKING DECISIONS,
USEFUL IDEAS.

They are Thought Containers. All you have to do is catch
one of the ribbons and pull it down to you, pop the balloon
and let the contents shower over you. Of course it doesn't happen at once, but it begins the process. You have to know **what**
to think about before the thought can be born. Thoughts are
slippery and hard to keep hold of, which is why when you get
a good idea write it down and keep it until you have time to
make it into something real. Then you can send it down to the
next level for pre-manifestation programming.

It works like a factory. The factory makes certain things,
they need to keep making them in order to survive and pay
the workforce. Someone gets an idea of how to make their
product even better; they think about it, draw out a design and
present it to the boss. If he likes it, it is sent to the production
department who make a prototype. If this works well it goes
into full production.

Think of Briah in these terms and you have the basic idea of
all manifestation. But it NEEDS that power of thought to get
it going and that can take effort. Ideas are numerous, but they
don't stay around for long and if you don't grab them other
people will. Ideas once created are free to go where they will,
if it is your idea you get the first chance. If you don't take that
chance then it will go to someone else who will. Once you have
the idea you can get the cloud to take you back to the doorway
and return to the physical level.

Instead of the clouds and balloons try thinking of ideas as
bubbles, thousands of them floating around. They are very fragile and you have to hold them gently and with care, and burst
them at the right moment to get the idea into your head. You
think this is silly? Then let me tell you that using a humorous
analogy like this will stay in your mind much longer than using
a repetitious method of memory. Humour is essential in the

art of magic... use it to entice thoughts and ideas into your grasp.

Some ideas are notoriously hard to get a grip of... when this happens to me I think of a farmyard full of ideas in the form of hens. Now hens are fast... and hard to catch. So I fix on one hen and chase it around the yard. As I do so the idea gets clearer and when I manage to grab the hen it changes into the idea and settles down happily in my head. Crazy, but it works for me.

If you prefer to do things in a different and more old-fashioned way, then try this. Think about the kind of idea you need and when it is clear in your head imagine a small seed in your hand. Think of this seed as holding the idea you need. Imagine planting it in rich earth and watering it with a jug full of emotion which you need to get this idea into your head. For several days continue to imagine yourself watering the seed. Then it shows above the ground and you can watch it grow into a plant.

Finally it puts out a bud and after that you wait until the flower bud opens and as you inhale its scent the idea comes fully into your mind. It takes longer that way, but it works. However the best ideas often come at night or in the early morning when you are half asleep. **NEVER think you will remember it when you wake up... you seldom do.** This is the best time for ideas but you must write them down. This may seem overly light-hearted to those of you who think magic should be always serious. Well sometimes it is, but magic is also full of fun and laughter and laughter in a temple or a ritual is a precious thing. It holds a special kind of power, the power of the childish heart, the innocence of youth and the joy of living.

Yesod in Atziluth

This is the level of pure desire, an overwhelming need to BE and to FEEL-SEE-TASTE-TOUCH and SMELL. It is the level of the God Name, Shaddai el Chai, the Almighty Living God in translation. Here Life acknowledges the supremacy of The Creator and adores it by re- creating itself time and again and encouraging change in the very crucible of matter by adapting to new and challenging environments. It is by continual discovery and the gathering of information, and by striving to understand the mysteries that surround us that we may offer thanks to the Divine.

At this level we catch the first glimpse of the Divinity Within. A frightening thought at first, but as we progress in our studies and deepest moments of contemplation we begin to understand. It is at such moments that Gabriel the Great Messenger draws near with His message. We wait, as once a young girl waited, breathless with wonder, afraid, yet full of an inner peace. The voice of Gabriel is like the silver trumpet he carries and the message is always the same... but it carries different meanings for each one of us.

"Seek not the God without, for the One true God lies within."

Mary heard it as a confirmation of the child within; we can hear it as confirmation that we are a living part of the Almighty Living God. It is in this way and this way alone that the Creator can approach matter... by living within His creations.

As I told you in the first part of our journey through Yesod, the word SUD means mystery and it is in Yesod in Atziluth that Seers have their greatest and most precious visions. Here they touch the Inner Divinity with a purity of sight so complete that it can demand the sacrifice of life itself. Few of the ecstatic saints live for long, and both Enoch and Elijah brought through great visions, but then were taken up into the greater life, and transfigured into living examples of what human beings can achieve.

It was at this level that Jesus of Nazareth achieved his Transfiguration, something that happens to us all on a lower level at the moment of Death. It is the moment of spiritual mating when the human soul unites for a brief second in time with the Primal Creator and in that moment comes the conception of new ideas, new understanding of life, new hopes for the future. Such power filters down through all the levels and into the spheres to manifest in Malkuth in Assiah. In this way ALL THINGS COME TO US FROM THE HIGHER SPIRITUAL LEVELS.

Throughout this exploration of the sphere of Yesod there have been many clues, many pointers to other and greater meanings of mundane things. Nothing is without its greater Self, everything around us has the same variety of levels in different states of Being. It is here in Yesod in Atziluth that we find the magical image of The Strong Naked Man complementing the magical image of Netzach, The Beautiful Naked Woman.

Gabriel brings the power and the Grace of the WORD... I AM and offers it to each and everyone one of us. It is the key that unlocks the mystery, The SUD, of this sphere and the mystery is this. That every living thing comes into being with a spark of Godhood within. The Point of God is our divine inheritance, the portion of treasure that the prodigal son begged from his father and then went on to squander.

This innermost point of Pure Light is the last particle of that treasure, the part that can never be lost. It resides within us. Where else would the gift of the God of Creative Power be but close to the creative organs? It is found at the point of the Coccyx. It is the Star of Light at the end of the Spinal Wand of Power. Where the Kundalini snake goddess sleeps coiled around the Spine waiting to be aroused by the Divine Fire of Desire. When the Naked Woman of Netzach calls to him, the Naked Man of Yesod answers. It is no accident that Gabriel approached Mary with a Lily in full bloom in his hand. The Cup of the Flower and the phallic Stamen in its centre are all the symbols we need to understand the meaning of this event.

Yesod in Atziluth is where the Divine gestates within us until we are ready to accept, as Mary accepted, the Truth of the Divinity Within. Yesod and its Archangel carry a message to all of us. As in the Quest of the Grail, an answer is required to the Message. Perceval missed out on his first visit to the Castle of the Grail, but got it right on the second visit. When The Archangel appears to us with the Message of The ONE we are faced with the same dilemma. A question:

I AM THAT I AM, WHAT ARE YOU?

It is a question we will face in every incarnation and when we get it right the World of Yesod in Atziluth opens up before us. What can we say in return? The answer is simple…

I AM THAT WHICH WAS MADE IN YOUR IMAGE.

This answer reminds us that the virtue of Yesod is IN-DEPENDENCE & FREE WILL. But even Free Will carries a cost as the prodigal son found out. It is a long hard slog back home.

Yesod in Atziluth – Working

Repeat the usual instructions regarding quietness, privacy and a comfortable chair with a supportive back. Begin to breathe deeply and slowly and with each out breath relax more completely. When you feel ready close your eyes and allow yourself to sink into a soft warm darkness. As you drift listen until you begin to hear the sound of waves, and feel a cool evening breeze on your face. There is a salt smell to the air and the slight taste of salt on your lips. Open your inner eyes and find yourself standing at the water's edge on a small beach. You are wearing a robe of deepest indigo and the silver sandals of Yesodic power.

It is night and everything is quiet and still. On the horizon there is a faint glimmer of light and as you watch a full moon rises from the water. It seems much larger than usual, its light more powerful and magical. As it continues to rise the pathway of moonlight begins to move across the water towards you until it touches your feet.

Drawn by the power of the moon you step on to the path and begin to walk towards its source. At first your feet are in the water but as you continue the path begins to slope upwards and soon you are walking above the waves and up towards the magical lunar sphere of Yesod. It grows larger and larger and now you can see that the path disappears into the moon itself.

You pause and look up at the glowing sphere then with no hesitation you step forward and pass within. The lunar light encloses you and sweeps you into a spiral of moving light. You swirl with the movement allowing it to carry you up and up through the levels of Yesod, from Assiah, through Yetzirah into Briah and onwards into Atziluth. For a moment you lie where you have fallen, dizzy and breathless as if you were some 5,000 feet up, though you are far more than that in magical terms. Slowly you sit up and look around you.

You are in a garden, but what a garden. Trees, flowers, bushes of every kind abound here. All are in bloom and their scent fills the air turning it into a pot-pourri of perfume that is as intoxicating as a fine wine. The fruit trees are laden with their burden and all of them wear birds in their branches and seem to be aware of them as both life forms and adornments. The grass is smooth and soft under foot as you walk on it. Amazed and awestruck you turn in a circle just looking and marvelling at the beauty of it all. If it looks like this in summer, what must it be like in autumn when the leaves change colour.

At once and within seconds every tree is wearing its autumnal cloak of red, gold, and orange. You gasp aloud at the richness of it all, then with delight in your ability to do so, you change it all back to summer. Then you become aware of something else… you are totally naked, yet you do not feel awkward about this. You are content, it is warm, the wind is just right, and there are no thorns or stones so you decide to enjoy being free.

As you explore further you find more surprises. Animals of every kind are roaming free. The deer are willing to feed from your hand, the birds come to your call and even those animals you would normally be scared of come readily to your side. The feel of a cheetah's sleek coat is such a contrast against the roughness of a mountain gorilla, yet both are content to rest by your side. The cheetah purrs while the gorilla gently pats your face. You resume your walk and soon there is a retinue of animal and birds following you as you explore this Garden of Eden.

You come to a lake where other animals have come to drink and wash. A lioness and her cubs frolic at the edge and the mother allows you to cuddle her cubs and play with them. The day seems to last forever as if it is waiting for you to tell it to end, but you are having too much fun here. The fruit is ripe and sweet, the water is clear and pure, you are in no hurry to leave this paradise. Then, you hear your name called and turn your head.

Standing there is a… Being of some kind, its form seems to change and flow into different shapes and colours. Only the eyes remain steady. Large and brilliant, grey/blue in colour. The Being waits as you get to your feet wondering who this might be. By now you are so used your nakedness you do not bother trying to cover yourself.

"Who are you?"

"My name is..............." the sounds are incomprehensible, but then it adds... *"In your world I am Gabriel. I see that you have found Paradise. I hope you are enjoying your stay. May I sit with you, I think you may have questions you would like answered. We have been watching you since you arrived and thought it best to give you time to explore."*

"Thank you. You called this Paradise, is it truly that?"

"For you, yes, it is different for everyone. We have someone who spends his time in a library, he has yet to leave it and see what is outside. He is so engrossed with the books he has not yet realised that his physical body died many years ago."

You both laugh, and then you have a thought... "Er, am I dead?"

"No, you are very much alive... as yet, but you have reached a stage where you can visit, look around, change what you wish to change, create what you wish to create."

"Is this where I will come when it happens?"

"If that is your wish at the time... but this is only temporary, a place to rest and think over the life you have had, later you will find within you the desire to move on."

"What if I have not been as good as I should have been... I mean... like... is there a Hell."

"Hell is something you make for yourself, as you have made this for yourself. Remember what you have done, re-living the regrets and the consequences that is often a bigger Hell than the one depicted by human artists."

"Is God here."

"You are here."

"No, I mean GOD."

"And I said 'you are here', if you are here where else would God be?"

"I don't understand what you mean."

"You are God, for God is within you, you and God are the same, made from the same light and energy. God gave up Itself to make Life, therefore All Life is God."

"Then what are you?"

"I was one of the first to become aware of Self, but we are incomplete for we have no knowledge of manifestation, only what we can learn from you."

"But you are an angel, you have powers I don't have."

"Power is nothing compared to knowing manifestation. I envy you, you will be greater than I am now, or any of my siblings born with me. You have the same powers, you just don't believe in them, or understand how to use them... yet."

"Do you watch over us as the stories say you do?"

"We watch you and sometime help you, but you forget to ask and we cannot help unless you do so, even then we have to work within the Laws of the universe."

"But you are there."

"Yes, we are always there. Are you ready to go back now, you have stayed here long enough and your body grows tired. It is hard to stay at this level for very long. I can take you back if you would like that."

"Yes please, can I come again?"

"This is your place, your paradise and you can come here whenever you wish, and you can change it each time or leave it as it is. Come to me and I will carry you back."

You come close to the Being and for a moment you can sense the form within the light and the great wings that stretch out over twelve feet in width.

"Oh, your wings, they are beautiful."

"They are not wings in the sense you mean, they are extensions of my spiritual substance that I can shape at will. Your tales of shape-shifters speak of this."

The wings enfold you, Strong warm and incredibly soft. There is nothing to hold on to so you just let yourself be lifted and carried back into the warm darkness. It feels as if you sleep

65

for a while and then with a start you wake and find yourself in your own physical body, but there is a perfume all about you as if left by something or someone from another time and place. Give thanks and a blessing and return to your own world. This marks the end of the Sphere of Yesod. Next time we will enter the Sphere of Tiphereth and the middle point of our journey.

CHAPTER THREE

THE SPHERE OF TIPHERETH

The Sphere of Service and Sacrifice

As Malkuth represents Earth, and Yesod represents Water, Tiphereth stands for Fire. This element has always fascinated humankind, it has been worshipped as something mysterious, sacred and a cleanser of anything seen as contaminated. This element is used to describe or represent the powers of Love, Passion, Loyalty, Fanaticism, Martyrdom, Desire, Lust, and any emotion that raises the heartbeat.

Fire does more than cleanse, it inspires and renews, destroys and injures according to how it is used and who uses it. All the elements work in the same way both for and against humanity. All contain certain powers of physical, emotional, mental and spiritual energies. As human beings we can use them for good or for ill according to our nature.

Tiphereth is also seen in esoteric Christianity as the Christ Centre. In occult terms that means any of the Sacrificed Gods, from Inanna, to Mithras, and Baldur to Osiris. Included in this category we would expect to find humans such as Joan of Arc, Thomas More, Giordano Bruno and the victims of the Witch hunts in the middle-ages.

On the Middle Pillar it becomes the balance point of that which combines the powers of the two flanking pillars representing the feminine and masculine powers. It is also a balance point between Malkuth and Yesod and Daath and Kether. For the purpose of this course of teaching it is the centre that encloses the Solar Powers on the four levels. The uplifted human having recognised the Inner Divine Self in Malkuth, and accepted the Presence of the Point of God within in Yesod, must now face the internal Solar Logos as the representative of the Primal Word of Being… **I Am**. This is no easy task and it should be approached, as should all magical work, with caution and as much training and prior knowledge as possible.

Tiphereth in Assiah

Tiphereth in Assiah stands for Service in all its aspects. Typically at this level we might think of nursing, medical, social services, the armed forces and fire fighters, teachers, etc. But there are many ways of serving and not all of them are immediately recognised. Wives and mothers, good neighbours, tea ladies, office cleaners and many others give their time and often service beyond what they are expected to do. Ministers of many different belief systems including those of the esoteric world and The Craft give time and service to their calling.

Time is a precious gift; it is literally **your life** that you are offering. Every time you do something for someone else you are giving them a portion of your own lifetime. When I was 13 during World War II, my father gave me one of the most precious gifts I have ever had. Money was scarce and he could not afford to buy me a present. But when I unwrapped his gift (in newspaper, because we had no fancy wrapping paper then) I found a homemade chequebook he had constructed from blank sheets of notepaper. Each cheque was for an hour of his time, just for me; we could go for a walk together, go to the library and read together, sit and just talk and he could answer the questions I always had for him. He was MINE for that time and no one else's, not even my mother. I treasured every one of them and used them sparingly and remember them still.

Service in a shop can make or mar a day. I have been a shop assistant in my time, I know how hard it is to keep smiling when your feet ache and the customers are demanding. But it was your job to make them feel as if they mattered. Today when I go shopping and the assistant does not stop talking to her friend while serving me, when the courtesy of a smile and a "thank you" or a "can I help you" is not forthcoming and when my change is thrown on to the counter instead of being handed to me, I tend to think kindly of the "old days" when good manners were taught from childhood.

The Virtue of Tiphereth is "Service to the Great Work". The Work in this case being that of lifting ourselves to a higher level of spirituality. Giving to a charity is a service, cooking a meal for your family is a service. Opening a door for a heavily loaded person, male or female is a service. It does not have to be a grand gesture to be worthy of a place in Tiphereth of Assiah.

The service given to an esoteric school is a higher kind of service. In the SOL people are sometimes asked if they would like to become supervisors. In this way they can repay the service offered by those who guided them through their own lessons. They are aware of the apprehension of sending in those first lessons, the eagerness of waiting for comments, and the pleasure of well-deserved praise. They are invariably influenced by the attention they received from their own supervisor and so the service is carried on. Because Tiphereth is the sphere of sacrifice there is always a price to pay. NOTHING comes without cost. Time, effort, extra study, dealing with problems of home, work, and family all constitute payment.

The higher the initiation achieved the more one becomes "A Servant of the Light". Thirty years ago the idea of dedication to a partner, a religion, a country or an ideal was an accepted thing, now it is becoming less and less. Many people want what they perceive as the glamour of magic but without the work and study needed to acquire it. It takes years in a university to become a doctor or an architect and this is acceptable. The same time spent in a study of occult science is seen as a "hobby". How sad that is.

Tiphereth in Assiah – Working

The difference with this working is that it must be done at night, so if possible take a short nap sometime during the day. The ideal time to begin the working would be just after midnight and in a room that is dark. Prepare yourself as usual then breathe slowly and deeply paying attention to your breathing and relaxing more and more with each out breath. Close your eyes and withdraw into the centre of the brain where the limbic system holds sway. Feel yourself sinking into the quietness and resting there. It is important to maintain wakefulness and not fall into sleep.

Begin by imagining yourself getting up and walking to the door of the room. Now turn and look back at your body. Try to see it as clearly as you can, take your time. Now pass through the door and make your way to the front door. There stop and look back and take note of what you see. Then move into the garden, or front of the house and again stop and look back. Don't be afraid, your body will be safe if anything should happen, you would be re-called immediately.

Now you are free from the psychic atmosphere of the house and may go where you will. Dress yourself in a robe the colour of golden amber. Around your neck is a Lamen or magical pendant shaped like a Rose Cross. Hold out your arms to the side and hold the image of an owl in your mind. Let that image filter down through your body and your form will take on the form of the owl. Lift off into the night sky.

You are looking for an open space, or woodland, a lake or river, a place where there might be some pollution. Use your inner sight and you will be able to detect the poison. The trees will appear dull and lifeless, the earth will seem as if it has been scorched, water will appear sluggish and dull, you will be able to smell the pollution. Every town or city has places like this. Search out wasteland where people dump old cars, cans, food and human waste and where nothing is done to clear it.

When you find such a place take your human form again and walk the perimeter trailing light behind you to separate it from the rest of the surroundings. If the area is too large, then section one part off and work with that first and then return as often as you can until you have cleansed it all.

Now standing in the middle of the selected area begin to open each centre slowly and with as much power as you can summon. First the Head, feel the top of the head open up and a Lotus flower emerge from it in the form of a bud. Now focus on the Throat centre seeing it as a brilliant Diamond. Next comes the Solar centre, imagine this as a Chalice made from a single crystal. Down now to the Genital centre and the image here is that of an open oyster shell in which lies a single pearl. Finally the Earth Centre, see/feel your feet and toes becoming like the roots of a tree with tendrils reaching outwards and down into the very heart of the earth where she is still untouched and clean. Now raise your arms, tip your head back and invoke for Spiritual Light.

I Invoke the Light that was in the Beginning and shall be until the End.

I speak of the First Law of the Universe which is The Desire to Become.

I summon the Creative Fire that was the first Divine Spark of Life.

I call on the power of the First indrawn Breath that became... I AM.

I cry out to the Nurturing Power of Binah that Her tears may aid me.

I offer to be a Channel for these powers that the Earth may be cleansed.

Hold this moment, feel the intensity of it, believe in what you are doing to the exclusion of everything else. Above you there appears a point of Light it extends down and touches the Lotus which opens up to receive it. The Light travels down to touch and illuminate the Diamond. It starts to revolve and as it does so the light it reflects shoots out in all directions. The main point of Light continues down and fills the Chalice with blood red Light that changes to gold and moves down again to touch the Pearl. It glows and becomes iridescent and like the Diamond revolves and sheds its light all around.

Now the Light touches the roots and tendrils to provide a path into the Earth. The Lotus fills the air with perfume providing clean fresh air to sweeten and cleanse. The Diamond shatters into a cloud of brilliant dust that covers the polluted soil and sinks into it. One particle remains with you and rebuilds itself into a new centre. The Chalice tips and spills its precious fluid into the ground to feed it and encourage new growth. The Pearl becomes the full moon and shines her growing power on the trees, plants, grass and the small creatures that live there. The power passes through the roots your Earth Centre has provided.

Hold the down-pouring of Light as long as you can, then you will feel it begin to decline and gradually grow less and less. Then it will withdraw up through the centres you have opened and return to its own level of Being, which is the Primal Spiritual level. Become aware of a circle of Beings of Light and Power that have surrounded you while you were working. They are the Ashim, the angelic Choir and the angelic choir of Malkuth the Earth. You have done a great service for them this night. As a human being who holds and is aware of The Point of God Within, you have brought down far more power than they are able to do. You have offered a great service to the Earth and they will not forget this. Beyond them stand another ring of Beings, larger than the Ashim, they are the Cherubim of Yesod, the Builders, they will help the Ashim to rebuild what was polluted. A third circle of Beings stands beyond the Cherubim. They are tall and majestic and wear crowns of Glory. They are the Malachim, the Angelic Kings of Tiphereth and they will overlook and assess your work.

It is time to close down beginning with the Earth centre. Withdraw the roots and tendrils from the earth back into the soles of your feet. Make the sign of the circled cross over them. Close the Genital centre as the oyster shell closes over the pearl and bless it in the same way.

Move to the Solar centre and the chalice offers itself to you. Allow it to tip forward and feel the warmth as its contents flow into you. Bless it in the same way and move on to the Throat centre. The diamond sparkles as you bless it and melts into the centre. Now the Lotus, bless it and see it close up into a bud and withdraw. Hold out your arms, look up and give thanks to the Light.

I give thanks to the Light that Was, Is and shall be unto Eternity.
I embody the First Law of the Universe for I AM that which IS and WILL BE.
I praise the power of the Creative Fire that lies within me.
I acknowledge the Sacrifice of the First Breath that caused all things to become.
I make offering to the Power that is Binah the Mother and bless Her.
I am grateful for the knowledge that enables me to be a channel for the Light.

The Ashim, the Cherubim and the Malachim bow in acknowledgement of what you have done and their blessing covers you like a delicate mist and they leave. Once more you take the form of an owl and return to your own place. You remove your amber coloured robe but the Lamen of the Rose Cross stays with you, an internal and unseen gift from the Angelic world. Taking on your human form once more you enter the house and move to the place where your physical body awaits your coming. As you approach it the centres flare up with light and encompass the physical form flooding it with power and energy. Look at yourself and know that the power you have used this night is yours to command again wherever you find a place that needs cleansing of pollution.

Now sink into your physical body, as if you were climbing into a soft bed. Rest for a few minutes for you have used a lot of energy. Then begin to breathe slowly and deeply, allowing each in breath to re-vitalise you. Open your eyes and look around you. Get up and stretch your limbs and walk about a bit to get the feel of your body again. Make yourself something hot to drink and have some biscuits or cookies or a piece of cake… something sweet to raise your blood sugar.

Do something ordinary, read a page or two of a light fiction book, watch 15 minutes of television, or record your feelings about what you have achieved tonight, then go to bed and dream. Do not do this too often, once, maybe twice a month is enough or you will overdo things. **Do not use this as an exorcism;** it is not for that purpose and you need to be trained as an exorcist to do that kind of work without severe risk to yourself.

Tiphereth in Yetzirah

Tiphereth in Yetzirah involves working with levels and Beings that are ephemeral, meaning that they do not hold the same form or shape on a permanent basis, but are continually changing. Imagine walking along a lonely road at twilight and round a bend in the road you come face to face with something that is nothing like a human form but more like a pillar with hundreds of eyes.

This non-human being changes from moment to moment because it exists in every sphere, at every level, at one and the same time. It exhibits colours you have no name for because they are beyond your ability to recognise. It is twice your height, knows everything about you including things you thought your mother knew nothing about. You can feel it scanning you like an x-ray machine.

No, this is not a scene from *Stargate,* or the *Twilight Zone* and neither Steven Spielberg nor Stephen King are anywhere to be seen. You are face to face (metaphorically speaking) with Raphael the Archangel of Tiphereth, also known as the Healing Hand of God.

Granted this is not an everyday occurrence even at this spiritual level. But it is as near as one can get using our terminology to what an encounter at the level of Tiphereth in Yetzirah might be like. I think changeable is the least one can say about this level. Not only is Yetzirah the Astral level of all the spheres, it has no real substance that is equivalent to material matter. It is, as I have already said, Proto-Matter, matter that has yet to be used or formed but which is available for the human mind to utilize. It is a level more suited to the art of contemplation than meditation.

Contemplation is different to meditation and is more along the lines of sitting still and watching an empty and slightly alien landscape until a symbol or a Presence of some kind appears. When that happens, allow your eyes, ears, and mind to observe it without trying to rationalize it. In return allow whatever it might be to do the same to you. This is an important step, as you will be using a similar technique in the next two levels.

You are not seeking to actually "know" anything. You are simply an observer who is also being observed. In this way you can learn more than you thought possible because your mind is open to what is being observed rather than trying to equate it with what you already know.

Don't question about what, where, how, or why. Just look and be looked at.

The main aspect of Tiphereth in Yetzirah is Dedication, and the definition of the word is given as "Devotion to a person, idol, god-form, use or object". For the purpose of The Great Work we use it to describe devotion to the task of perfecting ourselves as potentially Divine Life Forms. In Assiah we devoted the Path-working to the healing of the Earth and in doing so dedicated our work to helping Earth to survive the indignities we have heaped upon her. In Yetzirah the devotion is twofold.

1. The first is aimed towards understanding the full meaning of The Unreserved Dedication. This is asked of someone who is undergoing a Third Degree Initiation. Sometimes it is offered before this event, but it really only takes effect and comes into its full and true meaning at this time. Until then, although the offer is noted and recorded, it is taken as a potential offering that may or may not come about. All too often in the early days it is offered in a rush of enthusiasm that dwindles when the full impact of the work involved and the real meaning of the word Unreserved is finally realised.

2. The second is the Healing of The Wounded King, or The Sacrificed God, or in some cases a Sacred Place, as in the story of The Waste Land.

This second theme is one that is worldwide in myth and legend and in almost every Tradition though seen in different forms. We can certainly see it in the Arthurian cycle of the Western Mysteries. We can see it in the Christian aspect of the Crucified Christ, or the story of Inanna's descent into the Underworld. It is present in the stories of Orpheus, Mithras, Buddha, Chuchulain, The Oak King and John Barleycorn and in fact in every Great Hero/Heroine or World Saviour.

The Dedication is always twofold, that of the Sacrificed and that of the Sacrificer(s). This inner meaning is rarely understood and even less talked about, as most secular priesthoods prefer to dwell on the Sacrifice as the main participant. However to understand the incredible power that a willing sacrifice can generate, both aspects must be taken into consideration or the result will not be as strong as it should, or can be, and, may even become twisted over the course of time. But a discussion of this is not appropriate here.

Suffice to say that the Sacred Sacrifice must die in one of the traditional ways: by drowning, after being hit on the head and immersed in the water; by Fire as in the burning of John Barleycorn after the throat has been cut; by suspension from a Sacred Tree; or by dismemberment and the limbs being buried in the earth. It is important that their blood falls on to and feeds the earth. As you can see this relates to the Four Elements and the manner of death can be found in every major tradition.

I have spoken at length of the Healing power of this sphere and at this level, but it should be understand that this is not a miracle cure for all ills. That miracles occur is beyond dispute and I have seen cures happen when hope was not even an option. But Destiny plays a part in every life. We all come into Life with a purpose, whether we fulfil that purpose rests on how we deal with the circumstances that arise.

Bear in mind that this sphere offers three Magical Images. These are usually given as The Child, The Enthroned King and The Sacrificed God in that Order. I would disagree with that and for these reasons. It is only when the "God/Chosen One" is sacrificed that the power of the act begins to enter

77

the World Mind. Unless that act takes place nothing can come about, nothing can happen. What is ORDAINED MUST happen. Therefore it is logical that this image has to be the first. The Cleansing of the Sacred Earth that took place in Assiah, the working before this one, prepares such a space. Now, here in Yetzirah, the actual Sacrifice becomes the magical image of this level. In Briah the image becomes the revered and adored "King" enthroned and placed above all else. But, we are told in the Bible… "to enter the Kingdom of Heaven you must become as a little child". It is on this that I base my theory, and the magical images that are used in the next three pathworkings. It is your choice to make.

Tiphereth in Yetzirah – Working

Set free your astral form as you did with the last pathworking, dressed in a robe of rich salmon pink and wearing the angelic lamen and the silver sandals. Instead of taking the form of an owl you wait silently before your home. After a few short minutes a bright point of light drops from the night sky and hovers before you. Then it lengthens and widens and becomes a brilliant pillar of Rose and Amber coloured light. This light travels in a spiral up and down the column rather like an old-fashioned barber's pole. Near the top of the pillar is a ring of white light like a halo and embedded within it are eyes. Translucent trails of light float around the pillar almost like wings. Then a low and vibrant voice, sounds inside your head.

"I greet you Seeker of Light. I am to be your guide on this journey, allow me to transport you to the level of the dimension you call Yetzirah."

The trails of light wrap around you and lift you off your feet. Because they are wound about you, you cannot see what is happening but you feel a blast of icy coldness, impenetrable darkness then there is support beneath your feet again and you can see. Around you are high snow- capped mountains but beneath your feet is grass. You stand with many others but unlike you they are dressed in white. Some wear heavy collars of gold and strange head-dresses. Some hold trumpets and others have branches of green leaves that carry white berries.

An old man with a white beard steps forward and in a musical language that you cannot understand he declaims what you think might be a poem. It is long but its effect on those around you is dramatic. They close their eyes and sway to the power of his voice. Like an instrument it reaches into your emotions and though you cannot understand what is being said you react and begin to sway and stamp your feet like the others. Your companion lays a hand upon your arm.

"Do not let yourself be drawn in… you must remain as an observer, a witness."

You close down at once and discipline yourself to just be a Watcher. You become aware that you stand within a ring of tall stones. It is the centre ring of three stretching out into the darkness beyond the light of the torches held by many of those around you.

The declamation ends and the Trumpets are blown with great force. There is a faint light in the east and you realise that it is nearly dawn. Two white clad men enter the circle bringing with them a young girl of maybe 15 years. She wears a simple white robe with a white cord about her waist. On her head is a wreath of the same white-berried leaves you noticed before.

She is lifted with gentleness on to the flat stone in the centre of the circle and with growing horror you realize you are about to witness a sacrifice. You want to rush forward, to cry out to stop this happening, but you cannot move or utter a sound. Your companion whispers inside your head.

"Observe, and understand, they have not yet learned that blood sacrifice needs only one drop. But they will learn. She is calm and unafraid and goes with love as a willing victim. The one who will take her life is her grandfather. He gives his most cherished thing. Someone he loves. In this

there is a mystery."

As the first ray of the sun flashes between the stones the circle looses a cry of adoration in which the cry of the girl is lost. As the sun fills the sky you find yourself above the circle. Your angelic companion holds the girl, or rather her spiritual essence in its arms. She rests there smiling and unafraid. Others of the same kind as your companion stand beside you and wrap you in their arms and take you back between the dimensions.

The darkness seems endless but eventually you emerge into a large hall filled with torches. You know immediately where you are from the costume and headdresses. This is ancient Egypt. A tall man wearing an elaborate necklace of gold and jewels is speaking to the people gathered for the feast. Now he addresses another man wearing the crown of the Two Lands. There is a similarity between them and you know at once that this is Set and Osiris. You look for Isis and see her sitting beside her husband, but with alarm in her eyes, one hand at her throat.

Before them is a large sarcophagus beautifully decorated with paintings and embellished with jewels, the handles are gold and so is the small lock at the side. Set gestures to the gift he is presenting to his brother; you know the story, and you know what is going to happen, and instinctively you know that Osiris also knows it. You feel the presence of your companion beside you and turn round a question already on your lips.

"Yes, Seeker, he knows. He also knows that his death will bring sorrow to his people, his wife and son, but that it will in the end bring about a legend that will never die. He is a willing victim, look and observe."

You observe as the scene is played out, as you know it will be. You weep at the anguish of Isis but know also that Osiris goes with power. What stirs your thoughts however is the sight of Set striding from the Hall to slump against a wall in an empty corridor. He hides his face in his hands and weeps.

At your side the companion speaks and points. The bright spirit of Osiris stands beside his brother and murderer and places an unseen hand on his shoulder. Then his body grows brighter and brighter and dissolves into the starlight.

Next is Baldur the Beautiful struck down by the arrow of the Elected Sacrificer, and it is Loki the God of Fire who weeps.

Once more you are taken between the worlds this time to watch the death of Orpheus, torn apart by the maddened Maenads and his body thrown into the river. His lyre is broken into pieces and trodden underfoot. Adonis and Tammuz follow all taken in the flower of their youth. From there to ancient Scythia where you see a young maid go singing and dancing to her death, buried alive beneath earth that it might yield a good harvest. You are present at the deaths of Buddha and Mithras and each time you understand more of the Power of a Willing Death.

You stand and watch as the representative of John Barleycorn enters the field of corn with his bride who was his Beltane Maid. Now she carries his child and the sickle knife with which she will take the life of her Beltane Lord who is now the Lammas King.

She comes from the field with her robe bright with his blood and you watch as his body is bound in the last Sheaf of corn. He will be burned according to the ancient rites and his bright soul will fill the earth with power.

The last journey takes you to a garden where a man in a white robe walks with his friends in the cool of the evening. One stands apart, his face grey with grief. His friend comes to him and places his hand upon his shoulder and smiles.

"Do what you know you must, and do it quickly." The other nods and kisses him on the cheek. The darkness moves you quickly through time and now you stand on a quiet hill where three crosses are outlined against a stormy sky. There is a presence beside you that is far greater than your usual companion.

The voice however is just as low and vibrant.

"Do you begin now to understand the mystery of the Willing Sacrifice and its Cause? There must always be an opposition to maintain the balance of the universe. Without this there is no Balance and all will fall into chaos. I can tell you no more than this, the ultimate knowing must come from within."

You turn and look into the face of the Saviour of the Age of Pisces. Then the darkness claims you and you are standing once more outside your home. Enter and return to your physical body and make sure you eat and drink and close down firmly. This has been a difficult journey for you and it will have effects on your for many days. Rest now.

Tiphereth in Briah

It is at this level that the phenomenon referred to as the "Conversation with the Holy Guardian Angel" may sometimes take place. It is in fact a point of mind-to-mind contact with the lower levels of the angelic world. Don't mistake the word "lower" as meaning less important. It simply indicates a level where the human mind, or the Higher Self can begin to touch the higher worlds via thought power.

Just what is the Higher Self? It is another way of describing the Conscious Mind at the Briatic Level. As an analogy think of the way we enjoy literature. We all enjoy a good thriller or a romance as a way of relaxing and "turning off" the cares of the day. But then we also have to read things that pertain to our work: reports, training books, legal briefs, books recording advances in our particular area of expertise. But then there are times when we need something deeper, something that brings us closer to the wonder of the universe. This may be metaphysical poetry, William Blake's prose, or a biography of someone like the Dalai Lama. A book that makes us think deeply, ask questions and seek answers. It is this last that equates with

Tiphereth in Briah. For a Seeker in the Mysteries life is one long question mark. He/She is never tired of looking, learning, adding to the knowledge already there. There is no time to be bored even a time of rest means we can sort out things in our minds and prepare ourselves for the next day.

The virtue of Tiphereth is Devotion, another example of Dedication or Service, but on a higher level. The Higher Self is a part of the mind we rarely use or contact without training. Even then it is not something one can count on to happen on command. Contact is sometimes made when a really important realisation is made. But the moment is fleeting and often over in seconds.

Just before writing this, a student in Texas who works in the field of astronomy emailed me the following, she said:

"I have been l thinking about the Great Attractor;[2] I have had an insight. I was thinking about the Barycentre of the solar system and how it moves, though you can't 'see' it – you can only measure its effects, but this solar system and all those around it would fly apart without it – because they all revolve around it. It occurred to me that the 'empty' or hidden sphere of Daath on the Tree of Life is exactly like that. Everything revolves around it and nothing would work without it."

This is typical of a contact with the Higher Self. An insight into a known theory, but linked via the Higher Mind to knowledge concerning the way in which the universe acts as a Whole, with each piece fitting into place. What this student had done was to give an entirely new look to the presence of Daath on the Tree of Life. In such moments the Higher and Lower minds unite to give us a completely new insight into our knowledge of the Tree.

---

2 The so-called Great Attractor or Barycentre is a region of huge mass (equivalent to tens of thousands of galaxies) that exerts a gravitational pull on the surrounding galaxies. It is estimated that the Great Attractor would have a diameter of about 300 million light-years and that its centre would lie 147 million light-years away from Earth.

With regard to the idea of sacrifice that is ongoing in Tiphereth in Briah we find the concept of the "Offering of Self to the Inner Divinity". We have already spoken of The Point of God Within and at the level of Briah this can be transformed into an Offering of Personal Service to a Teacher on the Inner Levels. The buzzword for this is channelling, a description I personally dislike. There has been far too much glamorisation of this area of the mysteries, and far too many books written about it, 99% of them written by people who don't have a clue what it really involves. The most popular seems to be of the "You too can be a Channeller" type.

This is not true, not everyone has the right type of energy, or the right vibrationary pattern or even the mental attitude for it. Untrained use of this kind of work can damage the psyche and lead to physical and even mental ill-health. There are many types and levels of spiritual communication ranging from the ordinary trance medium up to Cosmic Seership.

Having said that, the ability is beginning to increase in humankind and more and more are being born with an aptitude for such high level communication. However it does require training and that training begins with the courage to offer oneself to the Light for consideration as a pupil under an Inner Plane Teacher. This begins with making frequent contact with your own higher self and once this is established it paves the way for a deeper level of contact with the higher worlds.

Tiphereth in Briah – Working

Use the same preparation as you have done before for Tiphereth until you find yourself standing outside your own home under a star filled sky. You wear a robe of golden yellow with the Lamen of the Rose Cross displayed. Before you is a path of light leading to an Archway. As you pass through you find yourself in a small temple obviously meant for Malkuth.

It is decorated with flowers and growing things and the altar holds fruit, bread, and wine.

Sandalphon the Archangel is waiting for you, his robes of green and gold fall in graceful folds about his feet and he wears a coronet of vine leaves and grapes in his dark hair. He offers you bread and wine and then takes you to a small door behind the altar and opens it. Before you is a moonlit road leading uphill. You hear the door close behind you and begin to walk. The smooth paving stones are well lit by the full moon above and on the top of the hill you can see the outline of another temple. You know with certainty that this is the Moon Temple of Yesod.

The way is now very steep and you walk more slowly, but the door of the temple is open and waiting for you is the Archangel Gabriel. His robes of indigo and silver blend in with the colours in the temple, and you marvel at the width of his wings as he spreads them in welcome. Here the altar is made from Mother of Pearl and on it stands an open shell with a single pearl inside. The light from this one pearl illuminates the whole temple.

Gabriel brings water and washes your feet gently and dries them with the hem of his robe then anoints both hands and feet with Oil of Frankincense. Then he takes you to a door behind the altar in the east and opens it and you see a road lit by a glorious sunset. Gabriel urges you through the door and closes it behind you. You understand that you are ascending the Middle Pillar to Tiphereth.

Ahead of you and gleaming in the rays of the setting sun is a golden castle with a tall tower and at the top of the tower is a small dome. As you draw nearer the door opens and Raphael in robes of amber and rose waits to greet you. As he takes your hand you feel his spiritual energy rushing up your arm and across your chest filling your heart with joy and wonder. He takes you up a flight of stairs to an upper room furnished as a temple. At the altar he takes from you one small drop of blood and places it into a chalice of wine.

Raphael takes the chalice and asks you to follow him. He leads you to a large hall empty but for an ornate golden throne on which sits a crowned King. You are taken before him and asked to kneel and make the Unreserved Dedication, but you ask why this is asked of you, you do not feel that this is the time to make such an important decision.

Raphael smiles and tells you to look again and you see that the king has the face of Osiris, of Orpheus, of Mithras, of the young girl, and of the Nazarene Master… this King is the Aeon of the Age crowned with the power of the Creator. You bow as a courtesy, but as yet do not feel able to give the Dedication. Raphael takes you to a small door that leads to a spiral stairway up to the tower. Round and round you climb until finally you come to the top and into the tower room.

The room is empty but for a mirror and a table on which is a sphere of light. Raphael places the chalice within the sphere and it vanishes. The Archangel then tells you to look into the mirror and leaves the room. You stand before the mirror and look into it but it reflects nothing but a dark void, then as if from far away a brilliant point of light appears and comes towards you then stops.

The object looks like a human brain but it is filled with a radiant light of soft blue and from it emerge tendrils of golden light that reach out towards you, touching you gently and attaching themselves to you. There is no fear in you, just the knowledge that whatever this is, it is a part of you. The tendrils burrow gently into your brain and you become linked to your Super-conscious mind, your Higher Self. Relax and allow the contact to come from your Other Self. Offer it a welcome.

This first time may be just a way of getting the "feel" of each other. If you make this a regular meeting then it will begin to fill your head with knowledge. When you feel you have had enough ask for it to withdraw. It does so slowly and carefully re-winding its tendrils of light and drawing them back into itself. Offer it the image of a Rose or gemstone as a gift and see it absorbed. Then it will leave the way it came. This working should enable you to train yourself to make contact with the Higher Self, but do not overdo it. Once or twice a month is more than enough.

Raphael comes to take you back to the Temple where you find Gabriel and Uriel. And Michael dressed in Golden armour. The altar now holds wine and bread and you share communion with the Holy Four. Then it is time to leave and you all descend the stairway and take the road back to the Temple of the Moon. As you walk you ask a question of Raphael.

"Why did you take a drop of my blood and put it in the chalice, and what was the sphere you put it into and where did it go?"

"That is three questions," says Raphael. *"The drop of blood is your signature and by placing it in the chalice it is preserved. The sphere is a projection of Daath where your 'signature' will be kept until you decide if you wish to make the Unreserved Dedication. That question will be asked again at a later time when you have more knowledge of what it means. It is not compulsory and if between now and the end of your journey you decide it is not something you wish to do, it will be returned to you. If you do make the Dedication then the wine will be absorbed by the Creator."*

You reach the Lunar Temple and enter; Raphael and Michael bless you then return to the Castle. You, Gabriel and Uriel light three candles on the Altar of the Moon, then you take the road back to the temple of Malkuth. At the door Gabriel blesses you and returns to the Moon Temple and you enter the Temple of Earth with Uriel.

Here Uriel places a mark upon your forehead, invisible to all but those who have taken the same path. Then you are blessed and leave by the door through which you came and stand before your own home. Return to your physical Body and close down securely. You have achieved more than you know and there is more to come. Return to full awareness and rest. Record your thoughts and feelings. Doing this means you can use them as information when the time comes to pass on your knowledge to those coming behind you. In this way knowledge is never lost and the light will be carried from generation to generation.

Tiphereth in Atziluth

Tiphereth in Atziluth is a time of Blending with the Higher Self. There is a difference between fully contacting it and communing with it. Now is the time for you to become a part of it. At this point the Seeker comes into contact with the last and to my mind most powerful of the Magical Images of Tiphereth. The Ascended Child of God.

As I have told you, you are a multi-level being. Your Mind can exist in time and space AND outside of both. Once you fully understand this your Mind can take you anywhere in the universe. Just know that your imagination will always first show you what you think you should see. Then it will show you what is real.

This is the point on the Tree where the power and passion of every willing sacrifice this Earth has known is contained. Every age has produced a Saviour. A man or woman who has taken on the task of hosting a particle of the actual Primal Core. They manifest on Earth in the world of Matter with this Primal Power deep within them. In this way they bring the Godhead into everyday life, living as a human being among other humans.

They come prepared to withstand the internal power of what they are and the burning brightness of the Primal Force within them. They come to die and die they must for it is impossible for a human body to carry such power for more than a few earth years. They die because humanity fears them, yet every time they bring with them something that will save the Age.

To this time humanity has reviled, tortured, and finally killed each of its Saviours. And still they come. They come because there must be a time, finally, when humanity listens, understands and accepts the lesson they bring. When that happens a fully Human Saviour will be ready to take on the mantle of the Priest-King. One who can guide all the life forms that fill this Universe. This will be the era when The Lords of Humanity take their place with the Lords of Flame, Form and Mind.

It is this hoped for future that inspires me to choose the Ascended Child as the highest of the magical images of this sphere. When the Sacrifice has been made, the message that was left behind in the form of teachings becomes a pattern for that Age. Its power colours the behaviour among humanity. The image it evokes becomes something to be adored, idolised and revered. Set up upon a throne and seen as The Lord and King of the World, something that was not desired by the Sacrifice. Gradually this image decays over the time allotted to that Age and new ideas spring up. In the centre of these new ideas, like the ancient images of the Holy Child sitting on the opened lotus flower, we see the Magical Child returning to its place of origin to gather strength for the next excursion into matter.

Every man and woman is their own God, their own Saviour, and always their own Betrayer. Only you can save yourself. The banner displayed so often on roadside churches declaring that JESUS SAVES, is wrong. He, like every other Saviour tried desperately to teach us to save ourselves, but only a few listened and he paid the price of the willing sacrifice.

The goal, the Grail is there in our myths and legends. But sometimes a myth speaks not just of what has passed, but of what is yet to come. The Grail is not so much a reality as a promise and a plan for what we can hope will finally be The

Golden Age.

You have chosen to walk The Royal Road, and once you set foot upon it you must continue to the end. Even if you were to stop now, the road would carry you along with or without the aid of these lectures. To understand this we must refer to the greatest teaching of all:

AS ABOVE SO BELOW, BUT AFTER ANOTHER FASHION.

All Saviours have their beginning in the spiritual realms. That spirit must inevitably descend into the material world to carry out its purpose. It cannot do so in its own form, but spirit can clothe itself with the denser particles as it traverses the four levels of each sphere of the Middle Pillar.

Then it reaches Yesod in Assiah where it can gestate partially in human form. It is too fine a material to keep this form for long. But it is long enough to give its message to those who will carry it into the maturing Age. This is the Way of the Saviours who DESCEND the Royal Road in the hope that a few of those they have come to teach will be able in time to ASCEND it.

We stand on the brink of a New Age with its promise and its dangers. Those who have kept alive the Light of Ancient Knowledge hope that this time will be the right time. Can we do anything to help? Yes we can if we are willing to train, teach, and shoulder the responsibility that comes with serving the Light. We can also offer to share for a moment in time the gut wrenching pain of the Saviour of the Age. That is the true and only reason of Initiation.

Tiphereth in Atziluth – Working

This will probably be the hardest working of all in this series. It will bring up emotions that may be hard to deal with. Remember you can stop at a certain point ONLY. To stop anywhere else may cause effects such as migraine, racing heart, excessive sweating or stomach upsets. All magical training works on and through the endocrine system of the body. If you stop at the wrong moment the chemical processes going on in the body may back up and cause problems.

However these are not serious unless you have a heart problem or a condition such as Diabetes or Asthma. In which case occult work of this nature is not a good idea for you anyway. You will need to set aside a space of time for two consecutive days, as the working will be done in two stages. By now you should be able to go directly into a working with little preparation. Begin with the breathing and relaxation as usual then, when you feel it is the right moment, set your mind free and project it into the darkness that comes before the light.

***

The smell hits you first. Rotting vegetable matter, human sweat and excrement, both animal and human. Your vision clears and you find yourself on a narrow street in India. The ground is hard beneath you, your stomach is knotted with hunger and there is pain. The pain has been with you as long as you can remember, from the time when your father broke both your legs with an iron bar. The twisted sticks that are your legs make it easier for your family to beg for money from the tourists. Today the pain is very bad and you just want to go to sleep and not wake up.

"I know a place where you can do that, and when you wake up you'll be able to run again." The voice belongs to a young boy dressed

in a clear Rose pink tunic. He has dark curls and his skin is brown from the sun. He holds out his hand and you crawl over to him. As you take his hand the pain goes away and you walk together away from crowded street into a pain free darkness.

When the darkness lifts again you are curled up on a filthy bed in an almost empty room. The men who paid to abuse you have gone and are now drinking with your owner. You think you are nine years old, but are not sure though you can remember being told that you were six a long time ago. That was before your parents sold you. Since then it has been a nightmare of beatings and men who pushed themselves into you time and again, hurting you, tearing you. Now you just lie and wait for the next one, maybe today you might get something to eat. It is cold and you only have a thin sheet to cover yourself. Clothes are not necessary for someone like you.

"I know a place where you can get something to eat, and some clothes, and no one will hurt you again; come with me."

Standing beside the rusty iron bedstead is a young boy in a Rose coloured tunic, he has dark curly hair. He holds out a tunic like his own and helps you put it on then leads you out of that room and into another one where there is a soft bed with clean sheets and pillows and a big soft cuddly toy. You curl up on the bed and sink into a deep sleep.

You hear an enormous explosion and feel a blast of heat and pressure on your legs and head. When the dust and dirt clears away there is silence around you. You remember being in a truck and driving along a street… you were going back to barracks because your shift was over. You were hoping there would be a letter from your Mum and Dad. Maybe there was news of your sister's new baby… a boy or a girl? Then there was this big explosion…

You try to get up but find you can't. You struggle to push yourself up but there is nothing to push with. You twist your head and look down… there are no legs and no right arm…

Panic bubbles up in you. No, this can't be happening, it happens to other men, not to you. You won't let this be real; you won't go home a cripple, no.

"It's all right, I know where your legs are… I'll get them for you and your arm. Would you like something to drink?"

The young Nurse can't be more than eighteen, but she is there and has water for you. She wears a spotless white medical coat and pants and has dark curly hair tied back with a Rose Pink ribbon, a brown complexion and a wonderful smile. She helps you to stand up.

"Come along there's a house just over there and you can rest up a bit, you've had a bad shock."

She leads you to the house and you wonder why you thought you had lost your legs and your arm. Silly of you, must be the shock. The house seems familiar, rather like your parents' house back home. You can smell homemade bread, apple pie and coffee. You sit down at the table and rest your head on arms. You'll just have a short nap… and then you'll get back to the barracks.

In the shattered and now silent street the remains of the truck and the scattered limbs of the dead soldier lie under the hot sun. You stand with the young boy in a Rose coloured tunic just the two of you. His face is streaked with tears and as he lifts his hands to wipe them away you see the nail marks on his hands, and feet.

He looks up at you and asks, *"Why didn't they listen to me, I asked them to love one another, not hurt each other."* Let the darkness cover you and carry you back to your own time and place. Return to your physical body and give thanks for what and where you are.

93

Second Day

As you open your inner eyes you find yourself standing with the young boy in the same Rose coloured tunic in the ward of a hospital. He smiles at you and says, *"Thank you for coming back, you can be of help to me."*

He takes you to the bed of an elderly woman. She lies with her eyes closed, remembering the days of her youth, though now she is old and alone and her time has come.

The Ascended Child, for that is what and who He is, tells you that she is remembering her husband when they were young and in love. They never had children so now there is no one to be with her. He asks if you will take on the persona of her husband and you agree. The Child passes his hand over your face and with a shiver of energy you change. You stand by the bed and take her hand.

"Margie, come on dear it's time to go I've come to take you home." You hold her hand and she opens her eyes.

"Will, Willie is it you? Oh my dear I've been so lonely without you." She rises from the bed, young and vital as she once was. The Child comes forward and whispers in her ear and she smiles and nods and goes with him, turning her head to say, "I'll be back in a minute dear."

The darkness sweeps over you again and this time you find yourself standing beside a car crash and again the Child is with you. Standing beside the car is a middle-aged man wearing a clerical collar. He is looking at his own body lying slumped over the wheel. He turns to you understanding that you can see him.

"I tried to stop and draw into the side, but the pain was so bad… at least I didn't hurt anyone else." Then he sees The Child and his face lights up. "Oh, Oh, it's true, it's all true, I was so afraid it might not be, it's been so hard at times to keep believing. Oh, thank God, thank God, you're real, so real." The

Child comes forward and holds out his arms. The Pastor looks down at the wounded hands and feet and bursts into tears and kneels before the one he has served for so many years. The Child raises him up and turns to you.

"Believe in me, and believe in those that came before me on the same mission, and believe in the one who will come after me. Thank you for your help."

Light surrounds him and the Pastor and becomes so brilliant that you cannot look at it. Then... you are back in the warm darkness and you know it is time to return to your own physical self. But, you have been left with a gift, the gift of belief. You have completed your exploration of Tiphereth and now for Daath.

CHAPTER FOUR

THE SPHERE OF DAATH

The Sphere of Truth and Integrity

Daath, we are told in Jewish literature does not exist, there are TEN spheres and not ELEVEN, there are TEN and not NINE. However if it is not there why is it named, and why is it shown as a dotted circle between and below Binah and Chokmah? Once something is named it has presence, once it has presence it has Beingness, once it has Beingness **it is somewhere**, no matter where that somewhere is.

Confused? Well most of us are when it comes to Daath. However there are a lot of theories and ideas and where there are theories there is bound to be some knowledge. Human consciousness is continually changing and extending as it adapts to new discoveries. So it is my personal theory that Daath is very much THERE, it is just that Daath's "THERE" is not our "HERE".

Well perhaps I had better explain that a little more.

Daath's dimension is not the same as ours, it just intersects it at a different angle and for a purpose that is not altogether clear to us at this point in our evolution. In depictions of the Tree of Life it appears to straddle the Abyss and that may give us a small clue. Perhaps it is a way across that barrier that, while we cannot actually see it, gives us an idea that it is close by.

Astronomers can tell us where a small star is, even when we can't see it, by observing the movement of other stars nearby. They either attract or repel each other and by judging those small movements we can say with a fair amount of confidence that there IS something there. So with the same amount of confidence we can surmise that Daath IS somewhere in the vicinity because of its effect on the other spheres of the tree.

Remember Indiana Jones being faced with the seemingly impossible task of getting across the abyss in his quest for the Grail? He had to trust, he had to have faith that there was something there. Then when he took that first step over the edge… there was the bridge. It is the same with Daath… We have to believe there is a way over the abyss in order for it to manifest.

NOW… Think back over all the spheres you have already travelled and observed… what have you learned from it all? I'll remind you. The basic lesson is this… **you have to believe in something before it can manifest.** Without belief, without Faith you will not get far. Daath is a test, a BIG test.

Daath is also a gateway, a terminus, through which all energy, power, intent and purpose has to pass BEFORE it can travel further down the Tree. Remember what the student in Texas said regarding the power of The Great Attractor? Daath is doing just that it attracts everything destined for the lower area of the Tree. If it is perfect it goes through and manifests, if it is not perfect it will result in an imperfect product. Daath can also be seen and used as The Great Hall of Records, the Library of All the Knowledge there has ever been and is to come.

If it is **acting as an Attractor** then Daath is holding the entire Tree together. A sobering thought but it gives us another clue as to where it might really BE. It could be that it exists **in all the levels of all the spheres at one and the same time.** It could also be the point where all dimensions meet. Kether may be the same thing but on a higher level even than Daath. So having got some idea of what and where Daath is, how can we evaluate it in terms of the four levels as we have done with the other spheres? Let's see what we can make of it.

Daath in Assiah

How does something that exists in a dimension all of its own present itself in a manifested world? Obviously the first answer is... with great difficulty. But is it possible even in a small way? The only way we are going to get through this is by lateral thinking. If we can't see it, and can't touch it, can it even affect us and if so how? In Assiah the only attribute we can fully apply to Daath, the only way we can briefly and tentatively contact it, is contained in one word, HOPE. You can't see it, touch it, hear it, smell it or taste it yet it is there. It manifests when least expected and when it does it lifts us out of the ordinary world and into a place that has no direction, time or even meaning. It is totally intangible, yet... it is there. When it does appear that is the time when miracles happen.

Such a Daath Moment happened a few months ago in a hospital in the UK. A young man was badly injured in an un-provoked mugging. He was paralysed, in a coma, unable to open his eyes, or even breathe on his own. Doctors warned his mother, "If he can't breathe on his own after a few days we will turn it off as there is no way he is can survive." His mother refused to give in. She called on friends and relatives, and they in turn called others. All round the world they rallied sending healing thoughts, energy and HOPE. Then the miracle began. First he wept. His mother said, "He's in there fighting." Then he opened his eyes. Within a week he was responding to touch. He tried to smile, began to move a finger and to breathe on his own. Now, months later, he can sit up, speak a little, and move the limbs they thought would be paralysed for life. His mother clung to HOPE. Her only reason was for him to live. Though he has not yet fully recovered he is on his way. THAT is Daath in Assiah. It is HOPE aligned with FAITH that can often create the phenomenon we call miracles.

At the level of manifestation Daath acts rather like a Terminus or the departure lounge of an international airport. So, because it straddles the Abyss, itself a mystery of another kind and another kind of existence, it can provide access to other dimensions, paths, levels, and maybe… if we can find the ability within us, to other universes.

Existing as it does in a state of "Not Being", when we enter it and use it as a basis for a working or a ritual we automatically enter into the same state for a short while. Providing of course that we know what we are doing and go about it in the right way. Once we leave the "knowable" spheres below the Abyss, for the "unknowable" state of the Supernals above it we need to proceed with caution. I hasten to add that caution should be taken in all these workings, but with Daath and Kether, this should be doubled.

On a purely personal level I have often wondered if this is the level at which the special people we class as autistic savants spend part of their level of consciousness. The same might be said of those geniuses such as the young Mozart, Bach, Einstein and others, for surely their various and wondrous talents must have their origin at a level ordinary folk like you and I have yet to find within ourselves. The real purpose of and the possibilities that may lie within Daath, to say nothing of its possible effect on the human race in the future, have yet to be discovered. In the meantime all we can do is to keep circling its perimeter and making cautious forays into its outer layers while keeping one foot on solid ground. But, nothing ventured nothing gained as the saying goes and with that in mind we can take our first tentative steps into the virtually unknown world of Daath.

Daath in Assiah – Working

Since it never hurts to remember that the spiritual level can also hold laughter let's take the idea of a departure lounge as our theme for this working. As with any journey we need to plan ahead as far as possible. Luckily we don't need to pack nor do we need a passport. But it might be fun to create one. The more one adds to a pathworking the more real it becomes. As an inter-cosmic time traveller I suggest a silver medallion engraved with a winged sandal on one side with your name beneath it and on the reverse side an engraving of our solar system with the Earth highlighted as a green stone. Now we can begin.

I remind you of the need for privacy and quiet and a dim light. Go through your routine of relaxing, paying attention to shoulders and neck muscles. Begin to breathe slowly and deeply, centring into that point where your bottom meets the cushion… ground yourself there and make a link between your mind your body, and the earth of which you are a living part.

Think of your name, see it with the inner eye as being written in gold and drive this sigil through the base centre and into the earth beneath you, make this your marker for the return journey. Close the physical eyes and open the inner ones. You are wearing a robe of silver grey flecked with tiny points of golden yellow. See before you a door with a notice saying in large silver letters:

DAATH
Departure Lounge

Leave the physical form and walk to the door and pass through. You are in a huge domed space, light and airy with many seating areas, It looks like any large airport on earth… but there are exceptions. The glass dome looks out to a vista of galaxies, large and small, some far away and others looking uncomfortably near. Around are the usual shops and cafes and many small transport vehicles that scurry to and fro carrying their passengers to their destinations. Before you is a desk with a smartly dressed receptionist. Apart from the fact that she has bright blue skin, a single eye and two pairs of arms she seems... normal. Her voice is quite cultured and she speaks any language you care to come up with.

She takes your name and adds it to what you take to be a computer, then hands you your medallion passport and allows you through into the lounge. As you enter a small robot scurries up to you and hands you an in-flight bag bearing a Winged Sandal Logo and the words "Trans- Uranian Time Traveller". Inside you will find anything you are likely to need on your travels.

You now have time to look around you and see your fellow travellers. It is immediately obvious that not all of them are human in fact very few of them are. But they seem very pleasant and friendly. As you sit and drink coffee you mention to the robot waitress that everyone seems to speak your language very well. The robot points out that your passport translates for you while you are wearing it and also enables you to speak in what tongue is needed.

A large butterfly-like creature floats past leaving the scent of newly cut grass behind it and just as you are going to ask where it comes from, a two seater vehicle draws up and your name is called by the robot driver. You climb in and are whisked away through corridors and other waiting areas to a large and very ornamental door with your name on it and a notice saying... PRAXIS GALAXY. 87 light years. Seleni System, 4th planet. M4 (Oxygen breathing Life Forms).

You get out and the robot vehicle tells you to go through and speeds off. You go to knock on the door, but it is already opening to display something that looks like a fairground chute. Not knowing what to expect you hesitate, then the door closes and you are sucked into the chute. You hurtle down, or round, or up, or maybe all of them. Sometimes you are upside down, sometimes sideways on but always moving very fast.

Colours and geometric shapes flash past until finally you find yourself right side up and standing in a glass box looking out on a fantastic landscape. The door opens and you step out on to a world so different to your own you can hardly believe what you see.

In a totally black sky there are two suns, one much smaller than the other. The larger one is yellow like our own but the smaller one is pale blue and they travel at the same speed across the sky. There are stars also but not in any pattern that is familiar to you. You seem to be on some sort of beach but the "water" is a pale yellow and the beach itself consists of tiny pebbles of a startling array of colours.

Further up you can see what might be called trees if they were green, but these are dark blue with leaves of silvery white. They have both blossoms and what you take to be fruit, both of a paler blue than the trunk. There seems to be no path so you just walk on through the pale blue grass and come at last to a vast space at the edge of the blue forest. You have the sense that this may be some kind of city.

Shallow depressions have been sunk into the black earth, some much bigger than others but all filled with opaque spheres of many colours and sizes. Some move from place to place others stay where they are. Some are in groups of varying numbers, some are single, others in twos or threes. The one similarity is a triple extrusion at the top that is almost flower-like in shape. The feeling grows in you that this is indeed a city and these spheres are intelligent, but how do you find out?

One of the single spheres approaches you and a chord of music comes from one of the flowerlike antennae. This is repeated twice more and with the third repetition you realise that you are being spoken to through the music. You take out your silver passport and the music becomes words.

"You are most welcome to our world, we have not seen one of your kind for many dances of the suns and then it has been through the medium of... (you feel the Being delicately sorting through your mind to find the right word) ah, you name it sleep and dreams. I am (an arpeggio of notes in a Minor key ripples through your consciousness) How are you sounded... your name?"

You speak your name and the Being translates it into notes... that come out sounding like a chord of music but with several flat notes. The Being laughs... a sound like scales being sung in a Tenor voice. "I think that would be better like this..." It sounds the notes again but adjusting them and this time it sounds better. You ask the name of this planet and in return get a flowing harmony that your medallion translates as "Two Suns Dancing with Grace". The Sphere indicates the space around you that is now filled with many spheres that have gathered to speak with you.

This is indeed a city and the spheres exist by, for, and through, sound. The three flowerlike appendages are specialised. One is a breathing funnel and the second is for the creation of sound; the third opens more fully at certain times of their day, which is 40 hours long, that is when they take in sustenance from the blue trees in the form of nectar exuded by the leaves.

You talk and laugh and exchange knowledge of each other's worlds. So welcoming are the spheres and so eager to know about you that you soon forget they are what you have always thought of as "aliens" and simply accept them as you would your next door neighbour. You learn that many of your world's greatest musicians have come to this place in their dreams. drawn across time and space to a world where harmony is the reason for existing. You speak with sadness of your own world's inability to know true harmony between people. One sphere offers the opinion that there are too many types of Beings on earth and all different. Here there is only one form and one type of food so there is no need to be envious or to seek to have more than your share, and the power of sound compels harmony.

As the suns pass directly overhead the whole planet rings with a single note and all the spheres stand still vibrating in harmony with the earth note. Then as it dies away they move towards the blue forest and take you with them. They cluster around the trees and the leaves begin to drip a clear liquid that has the smell of honey. The spheres absorb it through their food funnel and as they feed they vibrate a series of notes that, you are told, aids digestion. As their feeding ends you ask one sphere if they experience love and do they have families?

"Yes we love and mate and have young but because our life-span is far longer than yours, births are rare and only occur when one of us ceases to sing."

"What happens to those who no longer sing?" you ask.

"They go to the Twin Suns," you are told, "and there they sing in a different way." Your medallion chimes and the spheres tell you it is time to return. Too long under their suns' light could harm you. A large group accompanies you back to the beach singing a special song for you. The harmonies are to strengthen your ability to appreciate sound and you try to sing with them as best you can. Your willingness to try to use their "language" delights them and they ask you to return when you can.

The glass cubicle stands with the door open and before you step inside one of the spheres holds out a leaf dripping with nectar. You taste it and the flavour bursts on your tongue and flows into your system and for a few moments you are able to sing farewell in their language. The notes that pour from your throat offer love and harmony and the HOPE that soon your species will meet more fully. The spheres vibrate in unison say-ing thank you.

The door closes and once more you are thrown across the light years of time and space until you stand before another door that opens to reveal transport waiting to take you back to the terminus. There you hand in your medallion and pass through into your own world. Close down securely and record your journey.

Daath in Yetzirah

In the last working we used the power of Daath to visit a different Earth, it was Assiah in a very unusual form but it was STILL Assiah, the manifesting level of that planet. But now we look to the Astral and Emotional levels of Daath.

Daath and Yesod have a great deal in common for as I have already told you if you fold the Tree in half at Tiphereth you find Yesod fills the seemingly "Empty Room" which is one of the symbols of Daath, while Malkuth then equates with Kether... as it should for Malkuth is Kallah, the "Bride" who will one day be lifted to the throne of Kether to take her place as the Queen of Heaven.

So, if Yesod is the Foundation, the Treasure House of Images, and the point from where the Machinery of the Universe sustains that universe, it makes it a very powerful point on the Middle Pillar. So how much MORE powerful is Daath, the higher octave of Yesod? Furthermore, if Yetzirah is the natural level of Yesod what will we find when we enter Daath in Yetzirah. One thing is certain we will find a greater control of emotion available here in Daath. But finding it and learning to use are two very different things.

Yesod is the place where Thought forms coming from the Briatic level take on a greater intensity prior to manifestation. Daath on the other hand constitutes a bottleneck between Kether the Originator of Matter in its highest and most spiritual form, and the lower levels of the Middle Pillar where matter is destined to be fired in the crucible of Earth. So here we see Daath as a spiritual quality controller. Only the finest spiritual matter gets the chance to descend into form by passing through Daath and only Matter that has passed the test of full manifestation with all its agonies and pain will get through Daath on its way **back** to Kether to complete Unification with its Originator. Daath gets the last word on both lines of traffic! Which is why its Angelic Choir is the Seraphim or Fiery Serpents who work with Michael as their General in the Hosts of Heaven.

Yesod does the same thing on a lower level. If a Thoughtform does not have the power or clarity to withstand the rigours of Malkuth it will remain a dream in Yetzirah and never become reality. If we cannot control our dreams and perfect our ideas they get stuck in Daath and never materialise. So what realisation do we get from all this?

The fact that both Yesod and Daath are the Upper and Lower powerhouses, the Control Points of the Middle Pillar and the level of Yetzirah, holds the key in both cases. Why? Because, Yetzirah is the level of causation. Assiah is too manifested, Briah is all mentality and not always capable of the THRUST needed to guide MATTER in both directions and Atziluth is too fine to descend far enough without help. Ergo both Yesod and Daath in Yetzirah are the Keys to the Kingdom in both directions. May I quote at this point the words:

"Thy Will be done on Earth, as it is in Heaven."

And also:

"As Above so Below, but in another Fashion."

IF you have had enough training, and IF you are the stuff of which an Adept is made you will see in that last paragraph and the quotations, evidence of one of the greatest secrets of the Mysteries.

You will also understand that this is one of main reasons why Daath is seen as being extraneous to the Tree and why it is thought of as "hidden" or "not there". If one learns to control those two points on that level too much power could be manifested and that could be fatal in more ways than one if it is misused. Thankfully very few human beings have managed it and even fewer knew what they were doing or how they were doing it and so could not repeat it. Most have burned themselves out in the process or brought about their own destruction. Think Alexander the Great and Adolf Hitler.

On the other hand this is also the point where the "Christs" of each age become fully empowered to complete their mission on earth. Having done so they pass again through Daath on their way home to Kether.

Daath in Yetzirah – Working

This working is different to those you have already undertaken. I am going to ask you to take a whole day to prepare. If possible spend the day alone or at least with as little interaction as you can without causing undue trouble to others. At least half the day should be spent fasting and drinking only water. Prepare your place of working drawing the curtains and lighting a small tea-light, burn a little incense, preferably a light church mixture, but not too much or too heavy. Bathe and put on clean clothes. The need for privacy is even more important this time.

Begin as usual with relaxation and deep breathing and will yourself to sink deeper as you breathe until your heartbeat slows and you feel ready to build the images. You stand at the edge of an oasis wearing a violet robe which is the colour of Daath at this level. It is night and the stars are brilliant. Overhead a thin crescent moon gives enough light for you to make out the trees and the tents set up around the desert lake There

107

is a feeling of expectation and the night air is cool on your face and body. From afar you hear the sound of wheels and the jingle of harness then the sound of hooves and into view comes a chariot.

The horses are sleek and well trained and come to a halt at your side. The chariot itself is a wonder to see. It is made of a shining metal that is unknown in your time but which the Atlanteans called Orichalcum. It is engraved and decorated with signs and symbols that seem to glow of their own accord. The Charioteer is tall and wrapped in a dark cloak and hooded to hide his face. No word is spoken but you know that it waits for you and you climb up beside the dark figure. A flick to the reins and the chariot moves up and over the dunes faster and faster and then… the horses leap into the air. You gasp and hold tightly to the sides of the chariot. The charioteer in a calm voice tells you not to worry, that you can come to no harm on this journey.

Within seconds you are above the sparse clouds and climbing even faster. The earth spins away far below and there is a jolt as you break through some kind of barrier into a twilight world filled with strange forms that keep pace with the chariot for a while, then fall back as if unable to maintain the speed. Another jolt and you enter a sunlit world but with no familiar earth beneath, only a huge fiery sun that grows larger and hotter until you fear for your life. Then you pass over it and into a place of purple and indigo where fiery serpentine shapes gather about the chariot like a guard of honour.

Around you, you can see spheres of fire, light, and radiation that vibrate with power and energy and you recognise them as the spheres of the Tree of Life. The nearest one glows with pale blues, lavender and soft greys like mother of pearl. Then it spins away and the chariot races on to its destination.

Comets shoot past you, their tails like trails of fire against the darkening sky as they make their endless journey through the galaxies. The stars seem very close and so bright they hurt to look at straight on. The chariot begins to descend in long sweeping circles until it lands with just a slight jolt on what seems to be a plateau over-looking a deep valley. The charioteer descends and holds out a hand to help you.

Silently the figure leads you to the edge of the plateau, and after one look you reel back, your head swimming and reach out a hand to clutch at your companion. This is no valley but an Abyss that falls into infinity, an infinity filled with fiery stars and whirling galaxies that disintegrate into dust as you watch only to re-form into monstrous shapes that have no meaning to them. There is nothing the mind can hold on to only a madness that has no beginning and no end. An on-going round of self- destruction, chaos unleashed and attempting to manifest where no manifestation is possible or ever will be. You stagger away from the edge and sink to the ground. A terrible fear besets you for you know this is the Abyss that divides the Tree of Life. Why are you here? What have you done wrong?

The charioteer lifts you to your feet and points upwards to a vast empty space. Slowly from far above the stars are descending. They cluster together and begin to rearrange their shape. Out of their glittering substance a recognisable form takes place, a bridge made of starlight. As delicate as a dragonfly's wing, as fragile as a spider's web, as wondrous as a child's dream it comes into being and gently settles into place. Spanning the Abyss below it, it offers a scintillating pathway to Kether, the Sphere of Infinite Grace. You are entranced. But now a second gathering of stars drops down in the very centre of the bridge and another manifestation begins.

In the very centre of the bridge the star materials build a castle of many coloured light. Its walls are faceted like a diamond, and like that gem they reflect light in all directions. The turrets are tiled with sapphires and the windows are glassed with emerald. The doors are of gold and the steps are onyx and jasper. You stand entranced by the beauty of the Crystal Castle of Daath. You go to set foot on the bridge, eager to explore this fairylike building but the charioteer holds you back.

"But I want to see it closer."

Your dark companion shakes his head and points to the bridge. Now you see that there are many gaps in the bridge, gaps that mean a drop into the horrors below, what is more, those gaps move about continuously making it impossible to know where to place your foot safely. The charioteer speaks.

"You are not yet prepared for the way across, there is work to do before you can make the attempt. You have been allowed to see what is ahead of you so that you CAN prepare. Come now, it is time to return."

With your head still turned to the wonder behind you, you allow yourself to be guided back to the chariot and climb inside. The Driver flicks the reins and the horses leap into the air, but wait! They are no longer horses instead the chariot is drawn by four amazing creatures, glowing with light and all winged. A Man, a Lion, a Bull and an Eagle, it is The Four Holy Creatures, the Primal Lords of the Elements, that carry you back through the levels.

The charioteer throws back the hood and reveals the face of Metatron the Archangel of the Throne of God. The perfect beauty of that face will stay with you forever. You pass back through the levels of Time and Space to land gently in the place where you began. Metatron leads you back to the oasis and tells you to rest and prepare for the next journey. Then takes his leave and the chariot lifts off to return to its own level. You must also return to the physical level and think about what you have experienced. Few humans have seen The Bridge of Daath that crosses the Abyss fewer still have crossed it while in the physical body.

Daath in Briah

Briah is the level where that which has been created by the Primal Parent begins to become understandable... just. It is here that The Divine Plan unfolds in all its glory and wonder. Because Daath is the great container of knowledge, locations and ideas, when it is experienced at the level of Briah we might hope to gain some measure of understanding concerning the inner meaning of the Mysteries of the Cosmos.

At this level of mental energy ideas abound, they float like birds of paradise soaring, changing, drifting and waiting for someone, anyone, to reach out and capture them. This is the beauty and the power of Daath in Briah everything is here for the asking all you have to do is take hold of it. At this level all the great thinkers, and the little thinkers as well, find their inspiration. Inventors, poets, writers, artists are frequent visitors to this level. As well as those people who get a single sudden bright idea that changes their lives and often the lives of others. The mother who invented the first disposable diaper, the linesman who thought up the little gadgets that keep electricity lines from getting entangled in high winds are an example.

Business men and women who take a chance on a sudden "whim" that becomes a success are those who, in a rare moment of clarity see an opening and grab hold of it. However you must be quick, for these ideas do not wait around, they are actively looking for a place to rest, a place that will draw them down into full manifestation. If you do not catch and hold them they will pass you by. I can tell you from bitter experience that once you let such an idea go, it does not come again, but someone else will benefit. Ideas are much more than a collection of "what ifs". They seem to have their own form of sentience that makes them look for people who will make them into a reality.

Many years ago when my children were young my daughter asked me to help her write a story. After a lot of thought I came up with a theme that actually developed into a small book. I got so interested I spent months working on it. Then my daughter lost interest and I put it aside and forgot about it. Some five years later when looking for a book for one of my godchildren I came across a book with exactly the same name and the same theme. In fact it was 75% the same book I had in a box in the attic and had never tried to publish. I missed the chance to begin writing 20 years earlier than I did.

When my children were even younger (in the early sixties) my daughter had difficulty sleeping and the only thing that helped her was to cuddle a small pillow filled with lavender I had been given as a gift. I thought it might be a great idea to make up Rag Dolls and fill them with herbs and sell them as sleep aids for kids. I thought up a name for them, "Huggables". In the early seventies someone picked up the idea from the mental level and produced the same idea of herb pillow in the form of soft Toys. The name? Huggables! When you get a good idea USE IT, it may NOT make you a million, on the other hand… it may do just that, but you have to grab the idea and make it come into manifestation.

Thoughts and thought-forms are creative energy patterns that actively look for a way to manifest. They have to do that through the medium of the human ability to make real objects out of those patterns. They cannot do it on their own… **they have to have a human partner to help them traverse those last two levels of Yesod and Malkuth.** That means you, me and everyone else who has a dream an idea, a hope, a wish or a desire to create something that is theirs alone. THIS is what makes us DIVINE, and marks us as creative beings made in the image of that which created us in the first place. This is all about a potential Divine Being grabbing opportunities and making decisions that can and will alter your life and your future. This is Daath working at the level of Briah.

Daath in Briah – Working

Make the same preparations as you did for Daath in Yetzirah and stand just outside the Oasis waiting for the Chariot. The moon highlights the shadows and seems to make them darker than usual. The stars are brilliant and you get the impression that they are eyes watching to see what you will do. At night the desert grows cold and the stark black and white of the scene around you is emphasised by a cold breeze.

You hear the faint jingle of metal against leather harness, the night sky seems to peel back revealing an even more intense blackness through which comes the Chariot. The winged forms of the Four Holy Creatures are much larger than life and the spiritual energy that surrounds them crackles like summer lightning. Metatron wrapped in the familiar dark cloak brings them to a standstill and gestures to you to climb on. Once you are safely aboard the chariot begins to move again and races over the dunes, then with a suddenness that takes your breath away it rises into the air and up towards the stars.

The opening through which it came is still open and as you plunge through it you feel the familiar jolt as the levels of awareness change. For the first time you are able to take an interest in this other level and when the forms you saw the last time surround the chariot you look at them closely.

At first they seem to change form constantly but as you concentrate you begin to see shapes that are familiar. To make sure you count them... there are 22. They are Hebrew letters the Aleph-Bet. From your studies you know that, though they are thought of as letters, they are also divine beings in their own right. As they keep pace with you each one sounds a musical chord that holds the meaning of their letterform. You make a mental note to read more about them when you return. As you make this decision they melt away into the darkness and the chariot approaches the doorway to the next level.

You lean over the side of the chariot to look ahead, the Winged Lion, the Lord of the Element of Fire turns its head and looks directly at you. The golden eyes are full of the power of Love, for Love and Fire go together. Impulsively you reach out and caress the thick mane and the Being responds with a purring sound. Ahead you see the faint outline that defines the beginning of the great Abyss and within minutes the chariot has slowed down and stops at the edge.

As you leave it you notice that although the Holy Creatures are reined to act as a guide, they are not actually harnessed to the chariot itself. They lift and transport it by their own power. They take their rest as Metatron walks with you to the edge. Overhead the same stars begin their descent and you watch with fascination as they come together to form the delicate bridge you saw last time. Then the second group of stars come to create the Castle of Daath. You feel a longing rise up within you to cross the bridge even if, as you suspect, there would be no return to your own world.

Then Metatron takes your hand and to your amazement begins to lead you across. At first it is terrifying because the bridge is semi-transparent and you can see the Abyss far below you. You touch the delicate star built structure with wonder, it feels so fragile yet it also vibrates with stellar energy and power. The colours change constantly as if the whole thing was made from a diamond that reflects the light of the Spiritual world.

As you draw nearer to the castle you begin to realise how big it really is. Seen from afar it looked almost doll-like now you see that it is almost a small city in itself. You remind yourself that this is the manifestation of an entire Sphere or at least the nearest that matter on this level can get to a manifestation. You climb the steps to a massive door made of gold and engraved with symbols. Some you recognise and others have a feeling of being totally alien to your own world.

Metatron grasps a door knocker shaped like a hand holding a lightning bolt and knocks three times. The door opens silently and you pass within. The floor is tiled with black and white squares of onyx and marble and before you a marble stairway leads to the upper floors. All around you are statues from the ancient past of Earth. Any museum would be over-joyed to have such things. Metatron tells you that all these won-ders were made on earth and by human hands, but though they were destroyed the original idea and pattern remain at this level.

"Nothing is ever lost, everything that has ever manifested remains in its original form here, even if it no longer exists on Earth. But I have brought you here to see something else."

He guides you through a series of rooms and out into a garden that is in full bloom. Every tree and bush can be seen at its best. You are astonished to find that while the other side of the castle is under a night sky full of stars, here it is daytime with a warm sun high in the sky. The colours and the scents of the garden are almost overwhelming in their variety and strength. You go down a short flight of steps and walk among the flowerbeds.

You reach out and touch a flower and it sings out a note pure and clear, you touch another and hear a different note, but in harmony with the first. Totally entranced you move from one plant to another and each time you hear a note. Experimenting, you move in quick succession from one to another creating whole chords of music. Metatron laughs at your enjoyment and his laughter is as musical as the voices of the plants. Then you notice something else, something you know is not usual in a garden on the earth plane.

Some of the flowers, trees and plants have small closed buds and as these open they exude a sphere that rises into the air and floats away. You ask your companion about them. He reaches out and catches one in his hand and holds it to the light. You can see in its depths something moving. "Is it alive?" you ask?

115

"In a way yes, but not fully. Each sphere is an idea, a thought or a hope, a wish, a desire, or a dream. When they are strong enough they will descend to the lowest level they can reach and there they will drift and wait until someone can manifest them fully. If this does not happen they will be withdrawn and return here until the time is right for them to try again. This is also the place where forgotten knowledge returns to wait until it can be recalled and used again. See... (he catches a small sphere of pale gold in his hand and gives it to you). This is a memory from your own early days, take it and let it pass into your memory."

You hold the little sphere and press it against your forehead. It feels pleasantly warm and then it passes into your head and slowly a memory from your childhood begins to emerge. It is clear and sharp and very real.

"You can come here to remember things you thought you had forgotten, but if it is a memory that you are not ready to deal with, then it will return to its place until you are ready to experience it. Now come there is one more thing to see before you return."

He indicates a flight of steps leading up to a balcony surrounding the garden. Below you is another garden with wide lawns and trees, sand pits, toys, swings and everything a child could want. The place is full of children of all ages from small babies in cots and prams to older ones. Metatron explains:

"No this is not what I want to show you, but it is something you need to know about. These are children waiting to be born. Each one is a hope for the future. Some, like the spheres, will wander over the earth waiting for the moment of conception. Others have a destiny to follow and must wait here until the right moment comes into being. But now, this is what I want you to see."

You are led to another part of the balcony and from here you can see across the bridge to the other side of the Abyss. Here and there you can see people walking towards a bank of multi-coloured clouds and beyond them is a beautiful city. This city like the bridge and the Castle glitters in the light. A light that does not come from a sun but seems to emanate from everywhere simultaneously. At the end of the bridge there waits a being similar to Metatron. It radiates pure light. Afraid to ask, you raise your eyes to your angelic companion.

"Those you see crossing the bridge are on their way to Kether. There are four cities in that sphere and each one is more beautiful than the one before. The Being you see waiting to greet them is different for each person. They see it as being the Saviour or Prophet of their tradition. Very few achieve the final city, most spend many lives seeking to perfect themselves before they set out on the last journey. You are fortunate you have been given a chance to see as much as this. Now it is time for you to return."

With a last look at the mists that hide the city of Kether you follow him back through the garden into the Castle. The children still play on the green lawns and you wonder who they will become when they achieve full manifestation.

Back on the night side of the bridge you walk to where the chariot waits. You take a moment to bless and thank each of the Four Holy Ones for their willingness to carry you through the many levels of the Royal Road. Then you climb in beside Metatron and allow yourself to be taken back across the dimensions and back into your own time. At the oasis you again thank your companions and, then stand and watch as they return to the inner worlds of Light. You feel weary, yet filled with peace and you also have some knowledge now of what lies beyond the everyday in which you live and work. Rest now and let what you have seen become a treasured memory.

Daath in Atziluth

Atziluth means The Highest, the Absolute Limitless Light from which all things emerge. Daath means Knowledge. Combine the two and you have Knowledge that the human mind is, as yet, incapable of comprehending. Knowledge of what is beyond the Ain Soph Aur the Unknown Beginning. So how can we even hope to explain all this?

117

The short answer is we can't. But we can intuit, we can surmise, we can say what if? This is the way of humanity… even if we cannot hope to reach a certain goal it will not stop us from trying. You could say that besides HOPE, Optimism was the next best thing at the bottom of Pandora's box.

This is the last point in our journey where we can presume to know something concrete about all we have discovered during our journey along the Royal Road. After this it is all pure intuition. So where do we begin?

We can say that the World or Level of Atziluth itself can be seen as a source of Light that is constantly renewed, transmuted, transfigured and transformed. When you add the ingredient we call Knowledge to this we can begin to get the idea of a river of Information that is eternally flowing into creation from that unknown source. As it touches the beginning of what will become the Royal Road it begins to change slowly and gradually into something we will, or can try to understand. In other words it helps us to see knowledge, as an energy that can be changed, extended, made greater or lessened by the power of thought.

We then get a basic idea of how we can change the use of that knowledge according to our understanding of the sphere we are working with and what level of that sphere. To use a very mundane example… take cooking. We can give six people of different ages and races a piece of steak, some vegetables and a few spices and tell them to make a dinner. The results can range from a gourmet meal to a burnt offering worthy of a sacrifice to an ancient god form.

We can do the same with an algebraic formula, or mathematical equation. But different minds find different solutions. (in my own case it would be a disaster as I have never been able to deal with numerals). Out of all this the best I can offer as an explanation or a supposition, is that Daath in Atziluth is a constantly changing influx of knowledge that is disseminated throughout all the levels of each sphere in turn. Each sphere resonates to a certain type of energy and can use the flow of information to change and empower its particular energy so it can be used according to the nature of that sphere.

At this level very, very few people are able to work in a constructive way or even come near to being able to use it. What we can do is to **contemplate** it and intuit its power. We have to allow the Power/Light/Energy to reach a lower level before we can use, understand, or get near it. The good thing is that since EVERYTHING seeks to find its lowest level (according to the Second Law of Thermodynamics) this inflow of energy will eventually reach a point where we **can** use it but it takes a lot of patience and many years training even then. To try to use it before then is foolish and dangerous. Energy of any kind when misused can cause trouble; the energy of the Limitless Light could burn you to a crisp and may even be the reason why a few people have been burned to death inside their clothes, leaving their surroundings virtually untouched.[3]

One would not think about guiding a space shuttle without training and many years of expertise; working with Daath in Atziluth comes under the same heading. Even the pathworking for this level should be approached with caution.

Daath in Atziluth – Working

Prepare as you did for the last pathworking paying particular attention to privacy, quietness and cleanliness. Spend at least ten minutes relaxing and breathing until you feel quite sure you are ready to begin. Start to build the images with care and attention to detail. At this level your robe is of pale lavender. As the oasis comes into view you see the moon high in the sky, the brilliance of the stars and the faint glow of cooking fires.

3 Ablaze! The Mysterious Fires of Spontaneous Human Combustion. Larry Arnold. M. Evans & Co. 1995

Move away from the palm trees that edge the Pool and walk into the desert. The sand dunes throw long shadows in the moonlight and the sand is cold under your feet. The night air makes you shiver slightly. You stand and wait.

The Chariot arrives almost silently, with just the faint jingle of the harness. The Four Holy Creatures greet you by bowing their heads as you approach. You go to each one of them caressing the Lion's thick mane, running your hand over the sleek muscles of the Bull, and feeling the soft feathers of the Eagle's wings. When you come to the Winged human you extend your hands in greeting and they are grasped with gentle strength.

Then you climb into the Chariot and greet Metatron. He is no longer dark cloaked but wears a robe of deep Amethyst edged with gold and a circlet of gold around his brow. But as the chariot lifts into the air you see why he wears no cloak... his wings lift and spread out to a full six feet on either side white and blue and gold tipped they make a magnificent cover shielding you from the night air as you rise higher and higher.

As you ride you hear voices singing and look for the singers, but Metatron tells you it is the stars who are singing to welcome you. Then they are joined by the deeper voices of the Hebrew Letters as they surround you and add their own welcome. The great Archangel guides the chariot up and up and you wonder how you can still breathe and exist at this height, then you realise that it is the angelic wings that are keeping you safe and providing you with shelter.

You pass through the first barrier and you are surrounded by more forms of grace and beauty. The angelic Choir of this level, the Fiery Serpents of the Seraphim have come to greet you and keep you company as you travel. Their voices blend with those of the Stars and the Letters and Four Holy Ones who are also singing. A deep bass, rich in tone joins them and to your amazement it comes from the chariot itself. Metatron laughs at your surprise and tells you that here, at this level all things have form and voice and are capable of praising the Primal Emanation of the I AM.

"The whole Cosmos is alive and conscious," he tells you. *"Everything is one part of the whole and without that part it would be incomplete. You are also a part of that wholeness."*

You pass through into the next level and your companions are joined by more choirs. The Cherubim and the Malachim have also come to guide you into the level of Daath in Atziluth. The chariot glides over the Abyss and lands gently on the bridge itself, just before the Diamond castle of Daath. The Angelics fly over you, their wings beating the rarefied air and disappear into the cities of light on the other side. Metatron guides you to the door and bids you knock for entry.

"At this level you must do the asking," you are told. You knock three times and the door opens to reveal the black and white tiling of the hall and the marble stairway. But instead of taking the usual way you are now taken down a series of dark steps into a dimly lit passageway. This in turn ends in an iron ladder and Metatron urges you to climb down.

You find yourself among the latticed support of the actual bridge. A cold wind batters at you and the only footpath is narrow and dangerous. You make your way slowly and carefully along the stanchions until you reach the middle of the bridge and look down. Far below you can see forms moving to and fro and voices crying out. You look at Metatron and an unspoken question goes between you.

"They are the lost ones, those who must wait until someone takes pity on them and raises them up from the depths of their despair. They cannot understand that all they have to do is lift themselves from the depths. They believe they are being punished, but they are their own punishment. It is their own belief that keeps them there."

"Can we not help them?"

"You can, I may not for they do not ask and I can do nothing unless asked. But for those who tread this path and who come to this point the

grace is given that they may choose one and lift them up into the light."

"How do I choose just one?"

"You do not have to, you can walk away."

"Can I ask you to choose?"

"Yes, if you ask I can do that."

"Then please Metatron I ask you to lift one soul to the light."

Metatron spreads his wings and leaps down into the darkness below. You can follow his flight for his whole being radiates light. For a few minutes there is silence and then he re-appears his wings beating in long sweeping strokes that carry him up to stand beside you. He carries in his arms a man, thin and wasted his face etched with sorrow and despair, his eyes are closed and he seems to sleep. Metatron weeps as he holds him.

"What will happen to him now?"

"I will take him to the Garden of Children and he will become one of them and wait for a new birth and a new body. He has been given another chance. You must go on, you will find another ladder ahead that will lead you back into the castle and from there to the road that leads across the bridge."

He disappears and you follow his instructions and climb back into the castle. When you reach the ground floor you see a door before you. When you open it you find yourself on the other side of the castle and on the bridge.

Before you, you see the multi-hued clouds that hide the City and you run towards the end of the bridge. Hope and joy fill you as you draw near and then… standing before you with a drawn sword is Metatron and joy turns to disappointment.

"Not yet can you pass me. You still have some journeys to make but you have come far so do not despair. A time will be when you will come to this place to take your rest before re-birth. You have four more journeys to make before you can behold the Halls of Kether. To enter them while your physical body still exists is not possible. But take comfort in the thought that this day you have brought a despairing soul back into the light. Now

122

you must return."

You hear a sound behind you and turn... the Four Holy Creatures stand there and the Winged Human calls you to come to them. The Lion licks the tears from your face and they surround you pressing against you comforting you as they lead you away from the end of the bridge. Then they spread their wings and gather you up between them. Cradled with love and gentleness they take you back across the bridge and further through the barriers. The angelic choirs keep pace with you and sing you back to your own time and space.

The Four stand you gently on your feet and take their leave of you then return to their own level. For a moment you stand and weep, then you remember Metatron's promise and take heart. You pass through the quiet tents of the oasis and come at last into your own world to rest and sleep.

CHAPTER FIVE

THE SPHERE OF KETHER

The Sphere of Primal Emanation

Everything about Kether speaks of being THE FIRST Emanation. The First Moment of Becoming, the Point within the Circle. The Primal Parent. It is the barest hint of manifestation long before it becomes a thought or even a vague possibility. It has no comparison with anything else because there IS nothing else to compare it with.

The Magical Image of Kether shows a bearded male face in profile. Just the Right side of the Face is shown because the Left side still looks out onto the Ain Soph Aur from where the Great White Head originated. Maybe this was the very beginning of all those stories about the Left Hand Side being the wrong side, the bad side, the hidden side. As a left hander myself I am used to being called "wrong handed" though statistics show that left handed people are often more creative than their right handed counterparts.

Kether in Assiah

The one desire of Kether is to know the ultimate manifestation, to BE in every sense of the word. It is a Divine longing and yet it cannot be fulfilled. Why? Because the material of which the Divine is made is too fine, too im-material to become dense matter. Much as humans long to become fully spiritual, so does the Divine long to become fully manifest. Both still have a long way to go and trials to face before achieving their desire.

There is only one way we can both have what we want. We

have to find an intermediary that can act as a halfway house or host. A form that can hold both spirit and matter within itself and moreover, one that is willing to live for both and die for both. We need a form that can teach humanity about the blazing Divinity of Spirit, and teach the Divine about the emotional pain of Matter.

What CAN combine both is to be found in the Sacrificed Gods that have come to us in each age. Embodying as they do both the human and the divine they have come to us from the very beginning and continue to come and will ALWAYS come to teach, comfort, and embody truth until God and Humankind find a way to meld and become ONE: The Ultimate Wholeness of the Cosmos. In the bible we are told of the "Sacrifice made from the beginning of the World". A sweeping statement, but what does it actually mean? Perhaps it could mean this, and please understand that what follows are my personal thoughts only.

The Primal Parent despairs of being able to experience the fullness of Matter. It searches through the Cosmos for a suitable environment and builds the mental image of a life form to inhabit it. It endows that image with a particle of its own Divine Self in order that it may evolve and at a future time become aware of its Divine inheritance.

Suppose it then creates a spiritual version of that form with a similar Spark within, BUT separates that Spark from Itself for the lifetime of this cosmos. This form with the particle encased is now able to descend through the levels because it has, in effect been cast out into the universe. It gathers about itself layers of matter as it descends until it can incarnate. This new Life-form is very special, a Child of the Primal Parent in every way except one, it can take physical form. It was created to be The Sacrificed One in age after age. It would have been aware of its task and accepted it, for the Chosen must be willing. We see here the double aspect of Sacrifice. For a Parent to separate

Itself from a child and a special child at that and send it alone, to face such a fate, is a great sacrifice, as is that of the lonely spirit that must now endure an eternal task.

When such a Child takes on the Form of Humankind, then Humankind can begin to understand the complexity of Divine Power. But we are still left with the task of how to enable the pure matter of spirit to take on the dense and impure matter of Malkuth. It is a terrible choice and one that must cause spiritual pain, to leave the purity of the spirit and descend into an earthbound state. This explains the parable of the nativity. The Child must have supporters, one to give it human birth and one to guard its growing years.

The pretty story told to us in childhood of the Holy Child born in a stable amongst the animals is just that... a pretty story, but, like so many of the Midrashim of Jewish Tradition, it holds within a great truth. Being born into a human body after the joy of being pure spirit would be exchanging a palace for a stable. Born among the animals, of whom, let us not forget, we are just one species. Born into a human family to live, for a short while a human life.

The descent of the Aleph (the Breath of God) into the Beth (the house/form, or womb) explains the taking on of matter in order to teach Humanity about its divine origins. Aleph by the way has the magical image of an Ox one of the animals in the "stable". We might go further and upset the fundamentalists even more by suggesting that the story of the Fall of Lucifer is another way of telling the story of a bright, perfect spirit of Light, whose very name means "The Bringer of Light", was cast down into the level of matter as a SACRIFICED GOD. One who would bear the stigma and shame of being the opposite of God, yet whose descent would give humanity a choice and begin its climb back to perfection.

The brightest and most beloved of the spiritual hierarchy would surely be the one who would offer to carry this eternal burden, and carry it for humanity and the Divine. But there is another and deeper side to this. There can never be a Sacrifice without the Sacrificer. We learned that when working with Tiphereth. In the Descent of the Saviours we can see the determination of the Divine to manifest, and the equally strong determination of Matter to haul itself up into the Light. The "Saviour of the Age" is always the halfway point between the two, giving of itself to both even unto death.

We can see yet another version in the "Fall" from grace and the expulsion from the Garden of Eden. Ninety percent of the stories in the Bible are explanations of how humanity has been taught, pushed, coaxed, and bullied into a reluctant understanding of its divine inheritance as a Child of the Primal Parent.

We see it in the Tarot Trumps of the Fool and The Hanged Man, we hear it in the last words from the cross when the human side takes over the spiritual for a brief moment to ask… "Why hast thou forsaken me?" Having set the scene we can now make the journey.

Kether in Assiah – Working

It might be a good idea to do this working at night and to go to bed, alone, immediately after you close down. You may dream intensively or you may be exceptionally restless in your sleep. Have a thermos with a warm drink and something to eat to help you close down.

Go through the breathing and relaxing techniques as before and pay attention to the shoulders, arms and hands. When you feel ready close your eyes and begin to build the images. You stand in a lush field the grass is soft and slightly damp beneath your bare feet. You are dressed in a white robe flecked with gold and tied with a white cord. Stand and look up into the night sky. The stars are very bright and the moon is in her first quarter. Hold out your arms and mentally summon the Winged Bull symbol of the Element of Earth.

"Creature of Earth, great in your strength, I summon you by the earth within me. By the salt in my blood, by the minerals in my body, by the materials of which I am made I call you to me. I am of the earth, my body grown from the bounty of this planet. Come to me and do my bidding and be blessed by the divinity within me."

For a moment there is no response, then the ground beneath you trembles, you step back and the earth opens up and from its depths come a snort and a bellow, then the form of a massive Bull emerges from the earth and stands before you. As you watch it unfurls its wings until they stretch a full six feet on either side. Thoughts form in your head.

"Come Child of the Earth, climb upon my back and I will take you to where you need to go, you are expected. But first we must make a detour."

The Bull lifts a bent leg to assist you in climbing onto its back then it stamps a hoof on the ground and it open up again revealing a huge cavern. You are carried down in the depths where it is dark and damp. You come out into a vast cave filled with figures walking to and fro, some cry, some scream and some just stand silently and hopelessly.

"These are the lost ones, at physical death they have come here because this is all they can imagine. They have not been told about their ability to create. You are of the awakened ones you can help them find the light, if you are willing to do so. There are many caves like this, all full of souls that cannot find the light."

"How can I help them."

"Think of yourself as a Being of Light and that will attract them to you. Open your heart centre and call them in. It will be painful for they bring their fears, and troubles with them but it will only be for a short time."

You think about this, it is something you do not have to do, but the thought of leaving them in the darkness is something you cannot do. You open the heart centre and fill it with light. A great cry goes up. "The Light, the Light........." A rushing wind fills the cavern and you feel a pressure round your heart... your mind is filled with memories of pain, loss, abuse, fear, hate, and despair. It goes on and on until you feel you cannot bear another moment... and then suddenly there is peace within you and a voice that does not belong to the Bull.

"I am Uriel a Servant of the Most High and I thank you for this gift of love and light. Pass on now and bring those you carry with you into the Light."

The Bull spreads his wings and the earth opens up as you soar into the star filled space. Up and up until the earth is far below a shining sphere of blue and green. Beside you flies Uriel one hand resting on the horn of the Bull. Together you pass through into the next level and you can feel the panic of those you carry with you. You fill your heart with quietness and peaceful thoughts and the emotions quieten down. You keep your rescued souls tranquil as you pass through the second barrier and there before you is the Bridge.

The Bull lands gently and Uriel places his hand on your heart and those you have carried spill out into Uriel's hands in the form of tiny sparks and he carefully places them in his own heart centre. The Archangel looks at you and smiles.

"I will take them now to a place where they will be able to receive help. When the time is right they will be re-born. Because of you they will now be able to go on. Accept my blessing for this." He places his hand on your head and the warmth of it fills your soul with love. Uriel now disappears and you and the Bull go forward to where Metatron stands waiting.

"Greetings Metatron, may I enter into the city of Kether now?"

"You may enter the first Hall of the city but only that. You still have three journeys to take. Come."

129

He takes your hand and leads you from the bridge and through the misty clouds that hide the city from view. Before you is a building that looks rather like a Greek Temple. It is built of marble with pillars of onyx and green jasper and three steps lead up to the door. As you approach the doors open and you pass through into a great Hall that seems to have walls of pale rose coloured light. The Bull paces beside you but now it has changed and wears the head of a man.

Uriel comes to greet you with hands outstretched and smiling. He leads you to a row of three seats raised on a dais and invites you to sit on his right hand, while the Bull reclines on his left on a seat that adjusts to his physical shape and size.

Now into the Hall comes a procession of wonderful mythic creatures. Centaurs and nymphs, gnomes and dwarves, satyrs and fauns and delicate winged beings you think might be fairies. After them come tall beautiful people wearing rich garments of silk and brocade. Their beauty and bearing as well as their slightly slanted eyes and delicately pointed ears denote them as being of the Elven Folk.

You turn to Uriel with a question… "What are they doing here in this Place?"

"Did you think the Creator would turn His back on those who came before you? These are the Kindred of the Earth who have existed long before Humankind. Have you not been taught that all the created come from the One Creator? These life forms are as divine as you and your kind. They have a right to be here. When you cease to believe in them and relegate them to children's story books, they come here to wait until their time comes again."

You rise from your seat and go down to walk among them touching them, speaking with them, laughing with them. They hold no resentment at being banished from the earth. They speak of secret places where they still hold their revels and where those who still believe can see them. They fill the dreams of children and of those who retain their Child's Heart. They sing for you and dance for you and offer you fruit and small cakes made of wheat and filled with wild honey. You wonder at the strength of the centaurs and laugh as the fauns leap and caper and play on their pipes.

You speak with legends and dance with elves, tease the rough haired satyrs and chase the nymphs and dryads until you are exhausted while Uriel and the great Winged Bull watch and wait. Then a tall elf brings you a goblet of sweet wine and bids you drink. You return to your seat and feel sleep overtaking you. The Hall empties of Uriel's Children and silence comes stealing on feather soft feet.

Uriel gathers you up in his arms and mounts the back of the Winged Bull. Held in the arms of the Archangel you are carried across the levels of time and space and placed gently in your chair. **Think on what you have seen and realise that ALL creation is holy even if it is not human in form and Meditate upon this saying:**

KETHER IN ASSIAH IS MALKUTH UPLIFTED

When you understand its meaning you will have uncovered an ancient truth.

Kether in Yetzirah

In this sphere and at this level we encounter the Dreams of God. Does God dream? Look around you, this planet and everything on it, in it above and below it as well as everything else in the Cosmos is an integral part of God's Dream. When we desire something greatly, we say, "I dream of having a house with a big garden and maybe a swimming pool." We use the word and the concept of dreaming as a means of expressing a desire or a need we hope will be fulfilled. We are told we were made in God's image; that implies that we act, think, and have dreams in the same way, though at a much lower level. So a dream can be an aspiration, hope, a desire, a goal to be attained, or just a mix of sub-conscious ideas and memories that our brains need to sort out before trashing.

Yetzirah is the natural level of Yesod the sphere of dreams, mysteries, and desires so it is natural to use it to link Kether with the idea of a Creator who dreams of creating intelligent life, **life that will become His children.** The ancient Gods had many children, some by interaction with humans both male and female so there is a precedent to think that what is deemed to be The One God, the Creator of All Things would also desire to create in His own image.

What He created is… US, and we can take that further and say that all and any life forms, animal, vegetable and mineral can be included in this. After all children come in all shapes, sizes, and degrees of intelligence and talent, some, for reasons we cannot fathom, are not as well formed as they were intended to be. In the future we may encounter forms totally alien to our concept of "human".

Yesod is also called The Foundation, and **Life is the Foundation of this Cosmos.** A Cosmos created so Life would have a place in which it could grow to adulthood. It has taken a few million years to get there it is true, but then who's counting. Yesod gives the vision of The Machinery of the Universe and what could that machinery be but the ability to re-create ourselves in our children.

But why should a God with the power to create an entire Cosmos bother to create miniatures (in every sense of the word) of Itself, if there was not a greater purpose behind it. Could that purpose be to continue the dynasty so to speak?

What does a child require of its parent(s)? Comfort, food, shelter and protection are its main needs.

All animals, ourselves included, provide these things for our young. We prepare a place for their birth, we comfort them when they are afraid, we protect them from danger and we feed them from our own substance either through the production of milk or in some cases through regurgitated food (though milk could also be seen as a by-product of food ingested by the mother). How does God, as the Primal Parent do this for us at such a great distance? Or should we class the Creator as an absent parent?

Well we were given an entire cosmos as a "nest". In our own case an entire planet. We were given shelter in as much as primitive humans found caves in which to live and rear their young and certainly the earth provides, or did in the early days, a bountiful collection of food.

But once we had evolved into thinking beings and established the idea of religion, priesthood and a Creator God we began to use a very special kind of spiritual food. It began as a practice that today we find obscene, cannibalism.

When our ancestors faced and conquered a brave enemy it became the custom to eat the flesh and drink the blood of the slain in order to take into themselves the courage, and fighting spirit of the enemy.

This kind of practice was universal in the distant past. Then we are told of the advent of Melchisedek, the King of Peace, who apparently was without descent having no mother or father. (In other words a high ranking Priest who had renounced family life for that of the religious). He came to Abraham and taught him a new way to take the Godhead/Power and knowledge into himself through an act of transubstantiation, the changing of wine into symbolic blood and bread into symbolic flesh. The Nazarene Master used this ancient ritual to share himself with his friends and apostles at the last supper. We still use the same method today to take into ourselves the symbolic Christ powers of love, compassion, and the cleansing of the spirit. (INTENT is the magical tool of the magician, and the INTENT of turning wine into blood and bread into flesh is enough to make it happen on the higher levels.

All these things lead back to Yetzirah, the sphere of magic, ritual, dreams, transformation, creative power both mental and sexual, and the building of new forms. This is a very insubstantial sphere to deal with at an insubstantial level and you may find it difficult at first. Take it slowly and read the introduction several times and meditate on it. You may not agree with what has been said here, but remember what I have said earlier. In the main I am speaking of my own thoughts and experiences. You must not take these ideas as being set in stone. Learn to think for yourself. If my words give you the impetus to disagree with them and the urge to discover new ways of thinking for yourself, then I have been successful. Don't take the words of others as gospel unless they ring true in your heart.

Kether in Yetzirah – Working

As in the last working it is best to do this at night and to go to bed after you close down. Again you may find yourself dreaming about the working or dream of things you have seen. You may find some difficulty in actually getting to sleep. Have a warm drink and something to eat to help you close down.

Go through the breathing and relaxing techniques as before and pay attention to shoulders, arms and hands. When you are ready close your eyes and begin to build the images. You stand at the foot of a high hill crowned with trees. Behind you is a lake still and silent. You are dressed in a white robe bearing the symbol of a point within a circle. It is night and the stars are big and bright and appear close to the earth. The moon is in her second quarter. You climb the hill using a track made by those who have taken this path before you. It is steep and stony and your bare feet feel every stone and rock.

Halfway you pause and look down at the lake below and see the moon reflected in the water. You think back to the time when you first began this quest. It seems so long ago and so much has happened since then. You seem to have been a Seeker of Wisdom for so long. Then you turn and climb again.

Above you where the trees gather closely about the crown of the hill you hear a hard cry... the cry of an Eagle, and you increase the speed of your ascent. As you reach the first of the trees you hear the cry again. At the very top of the Hill you stand and hold out your arms and mentally summon the Eagle, the symbol of the Element of Water.

"Creature of Water, I summon you by the power of the water within me. By the trace of the ancient sea in my blood and by the rise and fall of my emotions and the ebb and flow of Life I call you to me. Giver and Cradle of Life I am of the primordial sea of this planet. Without you life would cease. Come to me and do my bidding and be blessed by the divinity within me."

The silence is broken by the third cry of the Eagle and the bird swoops towards you landing close by. It is many times larger than an eagle should be, but you remind yourself that this is one of the Four Holy Creatures that carry the Throne of the Most High. You approach without fear and caress the feathered head. The fierce golden eyes stare into your soul for a moment then the powerful creature leans into your hand and gently nibbles your fingers.

"You are not afraid of the Holy One Seeker, that is unusual."

The voice is unbelievably musical. Pitched low and with a quality of love and compassion never heard on the earth level. You turn and see Gabriel and smile. You had expected the Messenger to be here. He is after all the Regent of the Element of Water. He comes to your side and places his hand on your head. His blessing is like being under a shower of light and it pools in the moon centre of your astral body and goes further down into the passive physical form below.

"Come it is time to go, take your place on the back of the Eagle, you

will not fall I promise you, I will be by your side."

You do as you are bidden and find it easy to sit astride the Holy Creature. Gabriel tells you to hold on to the feathers of its neck. Then you are up and flying, you remember childhood dreams of flying with the birds and laugh with sheer joy at the sensation and Gabriel laughs with you. Far below the hill and the lake fall away beneath the mist and with a jolt you pass through into a world you are coming to know well. Almost without pause you pass through another level and look down on the gleaming bridge that crosses the Abyss.

The Eagle turns its head and sends a thought of welcome to you. You respond with a "thank you" in return, then land gently at the far end of the bridge. Gabriel helps you to dismount and the Eagle take off again. Together you and Gabriel walk towards the gleaming Hall you visited on your last journey, but to your surprise you are guided to the left along a broad street of mosaic tiles.

A few minutes brings you to another Hall, this made from black onyx and roofed with silver. Two Pillars of jade flank a door of silver, it opens at your approach. Inside all is dim and quiet. The only light comes from torches set into iron sconces along the walls. The scent of Frankincense fills the air along with the more subtle fragrance of Myrrh.

At the very back is a throne of dark wood on which sits the majestic figure of a woman. She is clothed in black and veiled but through the veil you can see on her breast a ruby pendant the catches the light of the torches. On her head is a coronet of stars. Gabriel goes towards the throne and kneels before it.

"Hail and Greetings Queen of Heaven, the Seeker comes before you and awaits your blessing and your words."

The woman beckons you forward and you obey, kneeling before her beside Gabriel. Power emanates from Her and a great sadness yet her voice is gentle and filled with compassion. She lifts her veil to show a face that is neither young nor old, simply ageless. The ruby now revealed is shown to be heart-shaped. It pulsates gently and you get the feeling this is her actual heart. Gabriel leaves you together and Binah the Great Mother, for it is she, draws you to her side.

"You have learned much on your journeys along the Royal Road. Soon you will make the last journey to the Hall of Kether itself. Only one more journey lies between you and that moment. Before then I am to give you some instruction.

"A recurring theme of your journeys has been to show you the power of sacrifice. You learned that the Sacrifice and Sacrificer share the same fate in many ways, that both must be willing to accept the burden such a thing requires. But, the Law of Three prevails. A Triangle cannot balance without a foundation, so there must be a third to share the pain, sorrow, and shame. I am that third, for I am the Mother of the Sacrifice. This is how it was decreed and how it has always been. The Sacrificed one bears the Pain. The Sacrificer bears the Shame, and I bear the Sorrow. But great as this Law is it must bow to another Law even greater.

"That which is Above is like unto that which is Below, but after another fashion.

"A sacrifice does not always mean the giving up of life. Your human life is full of sacrifices. A mother will give up small luxuries to give her children a treat. A Father will work longer hours even though weary to give them a better chance in Life. A brother will give the last sweet in his pocket to his sister, an older sister will help a younger brother with home-work. There are many forms of sacrifice.

"The giving up of a seat on a crowded train to one who needs it. The extra two ounces of meat slipped into a pensioners purchase by the butcher, the teenager who carries shopping for a pregnant woman. These are sacrifices of compassion, time, effort and strength. No matter how small, it will count. The Sadness felt on the death of a friend, relative or a pet will count. The gentleness of a vet putting down a badly injured animal will count.

"You think of the Inner Levels as being far away, but we are always close. What you feel, we feel. If We of the Above make the Great Sac-

rifices, it will never demean those smaller ones made by You in the Below.
Both will count on the last day. Now you must return, go with my blessing.
We will meet again."

She lowers her veil and Gabriel touches you on the shoulder.
He escorts you from the Hall to where the Eagle waits and you
take your seat again on its back. On the way you think of the
sorrow of The Great Mother and weep for Her. The Eagle
take you right back to where your body waits for you. You rest
your head against its breast for comfort. Then Gabriel gently
bids you farewell, and you return to your physical self to rest
and sleep. Meditate upon this saying:

KETHER IN YETZIRAH IS YESOD PERFECTED

When you understand its meaning you will have gained a
spiritual power.

Kether in Briah

Kether at this level is under the guidance of the Archangel
Ratziel who governs the sphere of Chokmah. He is the giver
of Wisdom and through him all new knowledge passes to Binah who fills it with the power of understanding. From there
it flows down through Daath and becomes knowledge in Malkuth.

Note that the flow is downwards towards Malkuth where
it becomes spiritual teachings of the highest quality. When it
flows the other way it is worldly knowledge gathered by human minds but not always understood. To gain that it must
go through Binah and on to Chokmah only then can human
knowledge truly become wisdom.

The greatest wisdom we can gain is the knowledge of ourselves as the inheritors of the Kingdom. "Know Thyself" said
the ancient sages, and then you will know God. We hear this

statement again and again throughout the writings of our ancestors and we still, after thousands of years have not accepted it. When called to initiation in Eleusis the final test was to face the room where God awaited the newly born initiate. After three days of fasting, meditation, repeated tests of courage and stamina, and long hours of ritual preparation the thought of facing some powerful God would have been terrifying. The initiate would descend into the cave beneath the great temple and walk along a dim corridor towards the final test. A pause before the door, a prayer for courage then the door opens.........
onto an empty room where the only thing in sight was a huge highly polished bronze mirror facing the door.

For some it was a puzzle... where was the God, were they unworthy? For others the emotion was anger at being duped. For those who had prepared well it was the moment of truth. God dwelt within, was found within, had always been within and would remain there.

When we talk in the Qabalah of seeing God face to face this is what we mean. This is perhaps, the reason why Metatron was transfigured from Enoch into an Archangel of the highest level. He saw himself, knew himself, understood himself as a mirror image of God. As we are told in Genesis... Enoch walked with God and was not!

Quantum Physics states that two identical objects cannot occupy the same space. One has to go or, be absorbed into the other, in which case something incredible happens and the power of the two become one and indivisible (it is called "entanglement"). The two now ONE, remain "themselves" in a way we cannot as yet fully understand (one of those times when we need the Understanding of Binah to convert Daath's Knowledge into the pure Wisdom of Chokmah).

We see a similar experience happening to Elijah, BUT on a slightly lower scale, if lower is the right word to use... Elijah is also transfigured into an archangel, (Sandalphon) but, and this is interesting, while Enoch/Metatron becomes the only one to see God Face to Face. Elijah/Sandalphon becomes the Archangel with a responsibility for Earth. Two human beings transformed into Angelic Beings and assigned to Kether and Malkuth, the highest and the lowest.

This leads us to look at the Vision of Wholeness, the concept that everything is linked to everything else. After all the entire Cosmos came from one Being, everything in it holds a particle of that Being. Every living thing, indeed everything per se, is made from that ONE. In the same way everything longs to be back with that ONE. The ONE likewise longs to become whole again but knows that if and when that happens those particles of Itself will have far more knowledge for they have known and experienced manifestation.

We sometimes touch that feeling of being one with the Whole. Waking early on a summer morning and walking on dew wet grass. Holding a wild creature in our hands and feeling its heart beating. Moments when we make love with that one special person. These are moments of wholeness. But we resist them, for to become part of a whole means we must lay down the self and become the many. That is very frightening for human beings. Individuality has been hard won. We moved out of the Group Soul into the individual Soul and to give it up seems to be a recessive move. Even the idea of becoming one with the Creator does not seem to be worth giving up personal identity. It requires real courage of the highest order.

Yet some humans have achieved it at least partially. Some of the saints like St John of the Cross, Teresa of Avila, Bernadette of Lourdes, Francis of Assisi. But I suspect that sainthood, and religious fervour is not the only way. I am convinced that the ordinary everyday human being can also achieve this oneness if not completely then partially. I think it may happen with those who live a solitary life of choice simply because it is what they want. A shepherd, a small farmer, a hermit or even a hobo meandering from place to place without a home or possessions can sometime be closer to this spiritual at-one-ness than those of us who live surrounded by "things".

The Knowledge of God and Oneness with All things. The voluntary giving up of the Self for something greater. This is Kether in Briah. The surprise comes when you discover that in giving up the Self, you find it again within that Wholeness... Untouched, complete, and so much more than it has ever been.

Kether in Briah – Working

Begin as usual with the preparation for privacy and quietness. Do this at night before sleeping, and fast for at least four hours before. Working on the highest levels of the Royal Road requires patience, dedication, and an inner serenity. Keep these requirements in mind. NEVER do these last four workings actually in bed or lying down, you MUST remain alert. When you feel ready close your eyes and begin the breathing sequence.

As your heart-beat slows and you begin to feel the approach of the Inner Levels relax even more into the moment, and build the images. You are on a wide savannah with the snow-capped mountain of Kilimanjaro before you. You know you are in Africa and you know who to expect. You turn your eyes to the mountain raise your arms and send out the summons.

"Creature of Fire, supreme in your majesty, I summon you by the internal fire within me. By the fire of my intellect, by the fire of creation in my physical body, by the Will of the Creator that called Life into being I call to you. Come to me and do my bidding and be blessed by the divinity within me."

Stand still and watch the sun go down over the mountain and as it touches the summit you hear the roar of the Winged Lion. It comes from the mountain with the fiery sunset behind it, illuminating it against the darkening plain.

It lands before you and roars its greetings. Unafraid you walk up to it and caress the great golden head. Its eyes look into yours and a blessing goes both ways. A rough tongue rasps against the skin of your hand. The creative fire of which it is the symbol calls to its counterpart within you and you look at your hand and for a moment it glows with inner fire and you can see the bones outlined against the light. The power within you stirs and gathers strength.

"You are learning to control the elements within you Seeker, that is good, but you will always need to be on your guard for any one of them can overpower you if given the chance. They are no ordinary elements, but Primal in their power and hold both sides of their nature in equal proportion: be aware of this."

You turn and greet Raphael the Healer. His robes are of the sunset colours and his face shines with the radiance of one who stands by the side of the Creator.

"Come, let us be on our way there is much to do on this journey."

You mount the great Lion and its wings stretch out and lift into the wind coming from the mountain. In long sweeping circles it carries you up until you can see the whole of the plain and the summit of the mountain below you, then swerves away into the darkening sky.

As you pass into the higher reaches of the earth's atmosphere the sky turns black and the stars become visible while the moon is poised on the brink of being full. You are so used to this kind of travel that you barely notice the passing from one level to another. Raphael, his wings of gold and amber beating steadily, flies beside you. You send a thought to him.

"This will be almost the last journey, what will happen after this? Will I be able to visit these levels again or will they be barred to me?"

"No, once given, the key can only be revoked by one far greater than I, and then only because of a misdemeanour so great the punishment would come from the Throne. You will be able to visit these levels as long as you

come with a pure heart and with the intent of learning more. Ah... we have arrived."

You have not even noticed the passing into the higher levels but now you see that the Lion is landing in the usual place at the end of the bridge. You dismount and thank the Lion and it settles down to wait until your return. Raphael directs you to the right of the Hall you first saw and as you go you ask your companion why there are no people, angels, mythical creatures or whatever to be seen.

Raphael explains: "*They are here, but as yet you cannot see them but they are aware of you. It will be different the next time you come and for that you must prepare well for it will take a lot of energy, will power and, yes, even courage to face what you will see. You may not fully understand it until a later time, but it will change your life Seeker.*"

He stops before a Temple of pale blue stone with a flight of steps leading up to an ancient wooden door. The whole building looks incredibly old and very interesting. Eagerly you climb the steps and knock on the doors. They open silently and the scent of old books, leather and polished wood envelopes you.

You walk into a vast ancient library. It is so much bigger on the inside than it looks on the outside. Raphael follows you and laughs as you stand with your mouth open looking around at the countless books housed here. There are also long polished tables and chairs, small spheres of light hover over each seat ready to illuminate the books. Here and there you hear the faint sound of voices and look inquiringly at Raphael.

"*Yes there are people here, there are always people here it is very popular, after the next journey you will see them and be able to talk to them. This is the Hall of Records, every word that has ever been written or spoken is recorded here and here is the one who rules it.*"

A tall austere looking angel emerges from a side room and come towards you. His robes are blue and grey and his wings are tucked neatly behind him. Like his fellows he is beautiful to look at but there is a feeling that he is not to be angered or disturbed.

"You are the Seeker?" You nod overcome by the majesty of this being. *"Then allow me to show you around. This is the main Hall of Records, but on each side you will find other smaller rooms where you can meet with teachers or contemplate what you have read. In the next hall leading from here you will find everything arranged first in age, and then in subject. You may not be able to read some languages but you can call for help."* He indicates a small bell on each table.

"I am Ratziel the Guardian and Keeper of the second Sphere to come into being. I expect you to be respectful of this place and those who work and come to study here. It is a place of Wisdom, or rather it is the meeting point of Knowledge, Understanding and Wisdom. Here is the beginning of everything that is new. Come I wish you to see the symbol of this place."

He leads you through the hall and into a space even larger than the first. It has a huge domed ceiling of coloured glass and the usual tables and seats arranged in a circle with shelves of books behind them. In the very centre of the Hall is a circular altar of stone containing a fire pit. As you watch a flame leaps from the centre and ascends almost to the dome itself, then dies down again. Again and again it flares up like a great fountain of fire.

"This is the eternal fire of creation, every new thought or idea is born here, each leap of the flame tells me that something new has been created. You are welcome here at any time, but obey the rules. Do not interfere with another person unless invited. You are unable to take books outside of the halls. Ask if you need help. There are gardens in which to walk if you wish." He leads you to a door that opens on to a lawn. In the centre of this space is a ring of ancient Stones covered in petroglyphs. Ratziel explains:

"This was the first temple ever built on your planet, it was lost to earth thousands of years ago but its original idea and concept remains here. You will also find all that has ever been lost here, statues and paintings, tablets and jewels and even the lost toys of childhood that were loved and

treasured. All have their place."

Raphael touches your shoulder. *"It is time to go Seeker."*

You thank Ratziel and bless him, he bows and watches as you are led away. Outside you walk with your companion back to where the Lion waits and climb on its back. Raphael bids you goodbye.

"I will not return with you this time. I must prepare for your next journey. Farewell Seeker and be blessed in your world." The Winged Lion lifts into the air and takes you back through the levels until you see far below the great African mountain. When you were last here it was sunset, now it is sunrise and together you and the Lion watch it come up over the wide savannah. You thank the Lion and Bless it and then will yourself back to your physical body to rest and sleep.

Meditate on this saying:

KETHER IN BRIAH IS TIPHERETH GLORIFIED

When you understand its meaning you will have gained the grace of the Holy Four.

Kether in Atziluth

We come now to the last journey, Kether at its highest level. This is rather like a Black Hole we know it is there, but we cannot see it or understand it. We will have to make educated guesses based on what we think we know. So where to begin? We could make a start by assuming that Humanity is a mirror image of God, since we are taught from childhood that we… "were made in His image". But it is also made clear that we can only meet with this Creator God after physical death. Heaven or Paradise is proposed as a possibility. But what does this mean?

It seems unlikely that our physical form could survive any kind of existence in another dimension or at a higher rate of vibration, based on what we know at this time. Professor Michio Kaku[4] the man most likely to know about other dimensions has theorized that there are at least ten of them. If the supposed Paradise is a planet similar to Earth to which we (well, according to certain tenets of belief a selected few) may be spiritually transported after death then that is another hypothesis and for some, equally unlikely. So we are running out of possibilities here.

Of course it may be that the physical does not come into it at all. So we are going to have to dip our toes into the waters of Quantum Physics again. This tells us that everything in this universe is made up of vibrating particles that come together in certain patterns and around a central core. One of these patterns is the basic human form. It also tells us that what we see when we look at each other is not what is really there. That it is an illusion (something the Buddhists have been saying for years). When their energy is used up these particle forms dissipate leaving a core particle which we may assume is the "soul" or God particle that contains everything that we are, have been or hopefully, will become. Are you still with me?

IF, as has already been stated we were made in God's image then we might assume that God is also a particle... but one far above us in Intelligence, Power, and Creative Ability. That would make a lot more sense than thinking of God as an old man in a white robe with a beard sitting on a golden throne somewhere "up there" in Heaven. Intelligence, Power and Creative Ability can come in any form. It does not have to have a head and four limbs.

A God Particle capable of creating an entire Cosmos is believable so is the possibility of an individualised particle be-

4 A Scientific Odyssey through Parallel Universes, Time Warps and The 10th Dimension, Michio Kaku. Oxford University Press, 2016.

coming one with its Creator and imparting to that Creator all the experience it has gained as a human form living in a manifested environment. It is becoming very clear, at least to me as a curious individual that Quantum Physics is what we used to call magic and it may well point the way to a greater understanding of spirituality in the future. It is too early yet to see where it will go on from here, but for me personally it has great possibilities. At the moment it is enough to say that "yes, we were indeed made in God's image", but just what that image is, is still under discussion.

In ancient times long before the coming of Christianity and certainly after that, Mystics, Seers, Oracles and Philosophers have held out the possibility of Becoming One with the Gods or God. They have spoken of The Wholeness of Life, and of the coming together of God and Its Creation into one glorious Whole.

In their moments of ecstasy the saints have spoken of it, poets have written of it, artists have tried to convey it in sculptures and paintings. All have despaired of even being able to speak of it in terms that us lesser mortals could understand. Think of Ezekiel, a wise man and a great prophet. To those who knew him he was the epitome of wisdom. Yet he could not completely convey the wonder of his vision. In his time the wisest would only have had between 500 and 1,000 words with which to talk, teach, and discuss the wonders about them. He described his vision with the few words he had, yet even today we still try to understand exactly what it was that he saw. But we can catch a glimpse of the emotion behind it.

He saw something that had no real form, yet had many forms that collaborated together to form a vision they wanted him to understand as best he could. He was shown a Wholeness of man and beast and objects. He called it the Throne of God. A Throne is something on which to sit, and from which one can govern. A Throne is also the name given to the angelic choir of Binah, the Feminine Supernal along with the gift of UNDERSTANDING. Make of this what you will.

If you follow the concept of the Big Bang, you know that according to this theory everything has come out of a single particle of immense density that is still expanding. You will also know that there is a second theory that eventually it will stop expanding and begin to contract back to that primal particle. Well, what have we just been saying about the return of the individualised particles returning to their Primal source?

I must emphasise here, as in other sections that all this is how I, as an ordinary human being see these things. I can present them to you, but you have to make up your mind or even turn your thought towards creating your own theories.

Kether in Atziluth – Working

So we come to the last journey. You have made nineteen of these journeys and this is the twentieth. Hopefully I have been able to share with you something of the wonder that I still find in such teachings after over fifty years of living with them day after day. For me the Cosmos is a picture book of beauty, information, instruction and sheer delight. So now it is time to reap the rewards of all your hard work.

Prepare carefully especially with regard to privacy and quietness. Any kind of interruption during this working would be a disaster. It is preferable to do it at night and to fast from lunch time, but have a hot drink in a thermos. Bathe and put on clean comfortable clothes or a robe. A candle and an incense stick are all you require. Offer a prayer of thanks to the Inner Plane Beings who have joined you on these journeys. Then begin to relax on each out breath until you feel ready to begin. Close your eyes and build the images.

As your inner sight opens all you see is Light in different colours, shades and intensities. Within the light forms are moving and coming towards you. Gentle hands touch you, tend to you. They remove your clothing and wash you with scented water and smooth oil into your skin. You sense you are being prepared for something important.

A tunic of white silk is placed over your head followed by a robe of blue velvet. A chain of gold links holding a medallion showing the heads of the Four Holy Creatures is placed round your neck and a golden cord goes round your waist. Soft sandals of leather go on your feet. Finally a cloak of blue velvet lined with white is placed about your shoulders and a circlet of gold is placed on your head. The invisible helpers draw back, and from the light comes a figure you know. Metatron takes you by the hand and leads you into and through the Light.

Before you is a road stretching into the distance, it is paved with marble tiles and each tile is marked with a name, for everyone who has trodden this road before there is a named tile. Urged on by Metatron you walk forward and the last of the mist clears away and you see the road is lined with people as far as your eyes can see. Among them are those you have always thought of as myths and legends, God Forms and the legendary creatures you met in your journeys along the great road. Also there are people you have known and met with in your worldly life and who have passed into the light. There will be others who, like yourself are still in this world and still searching, learning, and making their way along the road. You will give them hope that they can follow you.

As you walk slowly forward those who have come to greet you wave and shout your name and you feel both honoured and embarrassed by their delight. Ahead of you and standing in the centre of the road you see the Winged Bull with Uriel and Sandalphon. They greet you and turn to walk behind you. Flowers and ribbons and sweet herbs are cast before you as you walk and the scent of the crushed flowers rises like incense about you. Above it all you hear the pipes of Pan as the

Horned God the Guardian of the Wild Ones comes to take his place in your procession.

In the distance you can see a pair of Jade Gates guarded by two angelic warriors with drawn swords. As you draw near they lower their swords and bow and the Gates swing open to admit you and your growing entourage to enter into the Sphere of Yesod. The Gates remain open and the crowd follows you through. Here they are joined by your dreams, hopes, and desires who take form here in the World of Dreams. They all applaud you as you travel along the Royal Road. You find yourself remembering your journeys through Yesod on the four Levels.

They throw silver bubbles containing dreams before you and as they burst they give off visions of all the things you have dreamed of having in the physical world. It is their way of offering you dreams to delight your slumbers. Here to greet you is Gabriel and the beautiful Eagle that stands beside him. You greet them with love and tears of joy.

They join the others and for a moment you look back and find a sea of faces, a throng of well-wishers who have come to honour your dedication and your determination to complete the journey you began so long ago. This part of the Road runs through the world of The Moon and leads on to the Gates of Silver and Lapis guarded by two white Unicorns who bow their heads as you approach. The Gates open wide and the whole procession passes through into the Sphere of Tiphereth.

Here the sun is at its height and the air is full of singing birds and the scent of summer. Dryads and nymphs dance before you and the Muses have come to sing your praises. White robed druids, and Buddhists in their robes of gold and red bow and greet you as you pass. Hindu dancers throw coloured powders before you and their Gods smile and bless you. Austere Shinto priests sound their gongs and the People of the Wise place garlands of flowers before your feet. Every tradition and religion is here represented for this is the realm of Faith no matter what or how God is seen.

Rasta and Orisha drummers swell the crowd and everyone is dancing and celebrating, and it is all for you, to celebrate what you have done. As you come before the Gates of Gold an awesome presence stands there in full armour with a drawn sword. His face is stern but the eyes hold compassion. His wings outstretched hold the colours of the sunset. Beside him stands the Winged Lion. Michael, The Warrior General of God, closes his wings and sheathes his sword and throws open the Gates leading to Daath then joins with his angelic companions. The Lion comes to your side and offers a gift. A lion cub to become your own inner level Guardian, Its name is Shaka after a great Zulu Warrior King. Michael picks up the cub and carries it for you.

The Crowd fall silent as you travel the road through Daath. This is Hallowed Ground and all walk with reverence. Raphael and the Winged Human await you at the beginning of the bridge. They greet you and the Winged One gives you the Kiss of Peace. Then the Archangels and the Four Holy Creatures take wing and cross the bridge ahead of you. You notice the Castle has gone leaving just the bridge.

Beyond the bridge is a Radiance so great it hurts to look at it. But you know you must face it. You are not sure what to do, but know you must do something. The crowd is still, silent and waiting. You begin to cross the bridge and walk slowly towards the Radiance that you suspect might be what you dare not think it is. Far below you those who wait in darkness the hopeless ones, are also silent.

In the middle of the bridge you stop and look down, then back at the great procession of people who have travelled with you. You look towards the Radiance, then take off the crown, the cloak and the chain. Off too come the belt and the boots and the rich velvet robe. Barefooted and in a thin silk tunic you cross and bridge with downcast eyes and kneel before the Radiance that is Kether in Atziluth. The voice is deep and gentle.

"You do not like my gifts Seeker, you set them aside? Are they not rich enough?"

"Lord of Creation, how can I wear such things knowing what lies below, helpless and in darkness, and beyond hope. If I am deemed worthy of a gift I ask but one. Give those who wait below another chance at life for my sake as a child of the Most High and for the sake of all those who understand the meaning of sacrifice." There is a moment, an aeon of silence so profound that for a moment in time the Cosmos itself is still. Then comes the Word.

"So be it. Let them return to Life."

Heaven and Earth explode with joy, from untold millions of throats on a million different worlds comes a paean of joy, and the sound becomes a living thing that wraps you in love. You feel the hand upon your head and for a fleeting moment you are absorbed into what you know is GOD. It will never leave you now. You fall into pure love and rest there content. Sleep now and wake in your own time and place. You have walked the Royal Road and been crowned with love. On the Royal Road a new tile appears bearing your name and the symbol of a Bee.

When you wake, meditate upon this saying:

KETHER IN ATZILUTH IS DAATH IN EXCELSIS

When you understand the true meaning, a mystical name will be given to you in your heart. Use it in your work.

EPILOGUE

In many ways this is a personal story, begun years ago. Now, in my ninety-first year, I was clearing out old papers and came across a dog- eared manuscript and thought it might be of interest to those with whom I have shared the Occult Path over the years. During that time it has been my privilege, and delight to travel the world talking, sharing, laughing, and sometimes arguing over the many and varied areas of knowledge that comprise The Mysteries.

The quiet way of the Mystics, the curiosity and unrelenting search for knowledge and its eternally changing interpretations of the Qabalists, and the loving, laughter filled warmth of the modern Pagan Path, which in my humble opinion holds within its teachings some of the oldest religious practices of humankind have defined my life. I have studied, taught, practised, and shared in them all. I have worshipped (in my own way and without prejudice) in Hindu temples, Jewish synagogues, Muslim mosques, RC cathedrals, Stone Circles, Beltane Celebrations, Shinto shrines, Navaho Corn Dances, and Aboriginal Dreamtimes. But I keep returning to the Qabalah because of its (for me personally) Direct Connection between Humanity and the Creative Power of the Universe. I find its ability to fit in, explain, direct the mind, open up the senses, and alignment with other systems easy to use and deal with. So for better or worse, from the dusty shelves of my untidy and cluttered office I offer this book to anyone interested in my take on the Path of the Middle Pillar.

For those who think I have used the word "God" too often and Goddess not enough let me remind you that GOD has no gender, It WAS before there were two, which was when gender became an actuality.

This series of teachings has come out of a lot of thought,

contemplation and heart searching. For years I have studied and listened to those far wiser than I, pondered the results of my findings and even now I cannot see the end of learning. There is no end, for the cosmos is unending in its ability to renew and transfigure itself. For this I am grateful, I am also grateful for the opportunities this life has given me to know so many people of wisdom.

I have tried to pass on what I can. Remember that what you have here is of my own making, it is not taken from an ancient book of wisdom. It comes from my heart and my thoughts and my beliefs. Those beliefs have changed many times, for as I learn I change. Change is what magic really is. It is the ability to change yourself your life and your environment, and how you think. Gareth Knight once told me, "If you flow with change it doesn't hurt so much." There's a lot to be said for that argument.

If these journeys have helped you in any way, I am happy for you. If they have made you think, or even disagree, I am happy with that also. May Your God or Gods be with you.

Dolores Ashcroft-Nowicki
St Helier, Jersey. UK
June 6th 2020

Appendix

Colour Attributes in the Four Worlds

	Atziluth	Briah	Yetzirah	Assiah
Kether	Brilliance	Pure White Brilliance	Pure White Brilliance	White Flecked Gold
Daath	Lavender	Silvery Grey	Pure Violet	Grey Flecked Yellow
Tiphereth	Rose Pink	Yellow	Salmon Pink	Golden Amber
Yesod	Indigo	Violet	Very Dark Purple	Citrine Flecked Blue
Malkuth	Gold	Citrine Olive Russet Black	Citrine Olive Russet Black Flecked With Gold	Black Rayed With Yellow

www.ingramcontent.com/pod-product-compliance
Lightning Source LLC
Chambersburg PA
CBHW071222090426
42736CB00014B/2944